Two Jersey Brothers

Two Jersey Brothers

Stories from Our Haledon Boyhood 1939-1953

Nick and Bob Finamore

*For our grandchildren
Sabrina, Bobby, Kyle, Sarah,
Nicholas J, Caroline, Thomas
(TJ), and Robert;
and our wives Shirley Ann and
Marie Elaine*

Contents

Introduction

We attend an annual Festa Frainese at Holy Face Monastery in Clifton, New Jersey. The festival honors Santa Maria Mater Domini (Holy Mary Mother of God), just as it does at the Santuario di Santa

Mater Domini statue and altar at the Santuario di Santa Maria Mater Domini in Fraine, Italy.

Maria Mater Domini in Fraine, a town in the Abruzzo region of southern Italy.

Every June, just like our ancestors, we attend Mass and a procession of the Mater Domini statue, followed by a picnic with tasty Italian foods and music. We congregate with many families of Fraine heritage, including a cousin, Nicola Finamore, and another family member with the maiden surname, Marino.

The Società Frainese Mater Domini began the tradition thirty-five years ago at St. Michael's Grove in the Totowa section of Paterson, New Jersey. When those grounds were sold, the festival moved but continued. Participating is a way to honor our rich heritage, a source of great pride for both of us.

DNA testing shows Bob and I are both 97 percent Southern Italian, hailing from Abruzzo, Lazio, Umbria, Salerno, and Campania. The analysis makes

Finamore family photos

Left: Bob and Nick, circa 1943. Right: Nick and Bob, circa 1944.

sense: it covers the two major areas of Italy where our grandparents were born—Fraine in Abruzzo and Caserta in Campania.

While DNA is important, stories are what animates our family line going back to the old country. And so we write this book to preserve and present the stories of our boyhood growing up in Haledon, New Jersey. We recount the life we lived from 1939, when Nick was born, to 1953.

Though we collaborated on the whole book, Nick narrates most of our journey though Bob authored some of his own memories and experiences.

Our aim is the same: We write so our grandchildren will understand the era and hometown where we were born and developed our first memories, both happy and painful.

Morris Massey, past associate professor and dean at the University of Colorado, developed an intriguing theory that helps us understand who we become. His series of video lectures, *What You Are Is Where You Were When*, is based on the premise that we are sponges in our early stages of development. We absorb everything around us.

Later, up to age thirteen, we copy other people, often our parents, family members, and friends. At fourteen and fifteen, Massey says, our peers and the media highly influence us. We see ourselves as part of the world and develop our outlook on life. So what happens to us in our youth becomes a driving force in all we do.

We continue that theme. We write to show how our family relationships and circumstances in Haledon, as well as unforeseen events, shaped many of the choices and decisions we made throughout our lives.

Nick and Bob Finamore
New Jersey
Summer 2020

Prologue

429 Roe Street
Haledon, New Jersey
Circa 1938

Our parents, Nick and Teresa Finamore, met in school in Haledon, New Jersey. Many immigrants, including their parents, had settled in the one-square-mile town whose southern edge borders Paterson, then a leading silk manufacturing center.

Our parents, who worked in the same silk mill, married in 1937 at the Cedar Cliff Hotel and Restaurant on Belmont Avenue in Haledon. The newlyweds rented on the second floor of a four-apartment complex — two up, two down — at 429 Roe Street. The building had large front porches on the Roe Street side.

I was born on March 9, 1939 at Saint Joseph's Hospital in Paterson. Eighteen months later, brother Bob was born on August 15, 1940.

Finamore family photo

Nick and Bob's parents, Nick and Teresa, at their wedding at the
Cedar Cliff Hotel and Restaurant (1937).

My earliest memory is kneeling and playing with two yellow ducklings on the small back porch on Roe Street when I was three years old. The ducklings, an Easter present from my Uncle Tom Carnevale, were in a cardboard box. Experts tell us that we can have an indelible memory at that age or younger and that what we recall helps form who we become.

Bob: My earliest memory is standing on a rocking chair at 429 Roe Street, peering over a second-floor banister on the back porch facing Roe Street. I slipped, fell forward, and hit my chin. Since my mouth was open, I bit deeply into my tongue, which bled profusely. My father took me to the nearest doctor who, without anesthesia, sutured the laceration while my father held me down.

Another time neighbors were burning garbage a block away from our home. A particular tin can in the smoldering fire drew my attention. Not realizing the ashes were still hot, I grabbed the can and burned my fingertips. This very painful experience left a vivid memory.

During our early days on Roe Street, we continued having unforgettable experiences. One evening after dark, during a childhood game called hide-and-seek, I knelt on the sidewalk, hiding, with a dime in my hand. I didn't know what to do with the dime. Afraid I'd drop and lose it, I placed it in my mouth and accidentally swallowed it. My parents checked my stools for two weeks but couldn't find it. I'm certain it got passed. Could it still be there?

Another incident involved two brothers who lived near us. The family owned a store with an upstairs apartment. The father and mother traveled a lot, usually leaving the boys at home with a live-in caregiver and maid. One of the boys occasionally soiled his underpants. One day we saw the maid, yelling and running after the boy, his soiled underwear in her hand.

From the start Bob and I experienced a very diverse neighborhood on Roe Street. In a two-block area there were Italian, Jewish, Irish, German, Dutch, and Polish families, all with children who varied in age. Bob and I befriended many kids though the tough older boys bullied us younger ones. Their nicknames were unique — "Huck," "Carrot Top," "Lucky." Some were disruptive in school and had to stay after dismissal.

Living on Roe Street with other blue-collar families reflected our socioeconomic situation as a young family in the 1940s. My father bought a Model A two-seat roadster with a rumble seat, often called a "mother-in-law seat," in the back. It folded down into the rear trunk and had no cover. On one Sunday drive my brother and I were placed in that seat. There were no seat belts in those days! We broke down on High Mountain Road near Oldham Pond. A friend of my parents picked us up. The car was towed to a nearby gas station for repair.

Later in the '40s, my parents bought a used 1938 Plymouth Coupe with a waterfall grille and "bug-eyed" headlamps on either side of the radiator grille. It looked downright plump, pudgy, and kind of ugly. Its features included a long gear shift that emanated from the floor; a high beam button on the left driver's side floor, next to the manual shift clutch; running boards on each side; and locking vent front windows.

We didn't have a lot of money then. Our apartment used steam heat radiators, fueled by a coal-fired furnace in the basement. Several times a day, including the middle of the night, my father shoveled coal into the furnace to keep the fire going. We got a ton of coal delivered right into the basement via a coal chute through a window. The coal bin was extremely dusty — not a very healthy environment.

At least we had heat, though. My parents provided for us. They came through, as had their parents, all Italian immigrants who'd also seen hard times.

Two Jersey Brothers

Chapter 1
Small Town, Big History

The first European explorer who saw the land that later became Haledon probably was Henry Hudson. In 1609 the English explorer anchored his small ship, the *Half Moon*, off Manhattan Island. He sent two scouts ashore to find the Northwest Passage, a legendary waterway that would carry the ship from the Atlantic to the Pacific.

The pair reported a "great mountain" they'd seen in the distance—a mountain that might provide the view they needed. Many believe they found Haledon's High Mountain.

A century later in 1702, East and West Jersey were combined, creating the Colony of New Jersey. The first pioneers in what is now northern New Jersey were the Ryersons, Westervelts, and Van Houtens. In 1709 the Ryersons and Uria Westervelt secured 1,425 acres of land, including all of Haledon, from the American

Indians — to the best of our understanding, the Nanticoke Lenni-Lenapes.

When New Jersey became the third state to ratify the Constitution in 1787, Passaic County was formed and divided into five townships, including Manchester Township, which contained six towns. It would take until 1908 for the last town, Haledon, to separate from Manchester.

Originally, the town, once called Oldham and Deer Hill, was settled predominantly by farmers of Dutch heritage. The population grew as immigrants, mostly skilled European silk workers, arrived. The town held residential appeal; to live there was to escape crowded, industrial Paterson but still have access to its silk mills by trolley.

Trolley Days

The Horse Railroad Co., founded in 1871, laid trolley tracks along current-day Belmont Avenue from Paterson to Haledon. Horses pulled the original trollies, clip-clopping back and forth on the Belgian block routes until 1888.

They were replaced by electric trollies that drew power from overhead wires using trolley poles. Two wires and two poles were required to complete the electric circuit. The new trollies eliminated the problems of animal maintenance and horse manure, which had to constantly be cleaned from the street.

During peak times the goal was to have a trolley come through every eight to twelve minutes.

Many of the trolley company owners founded the Cedar Cliff Land Company and bought large portions of the area. The company targeted upwardly mobile silk workers with 25' x 100' tracts in Haledon. Cedar Cliff's ability to sell cheap land in such small sizes enabled people to buy their own home and garden. The company's sales slogan was "Get a Slice of the Earth." It set up tents and offered free breakfast or lunch to attract buyers.

In the 1890s, Cedar Cliff added three new silk mills as well as dye houses, all in Haledon.[1]

In the early 1900s, Haledon was a major streetcar hub to Paterson. In 1907 Public Service took over the electric trolley company and operated the line until they abandoned the streetcars in favor of bus lines.

In 1908 the town incorporated and took the name Haledon, after a town in England. It adopted a borough form of municipal government, meaning its mayor, elected directly by the people, serves a four-year term, and its six Borough Council members each get three-year terms.

Haledon street names read like a who's who of Paterson industry and commerce. John Calvin Roe was an early settler before the Civil War. Of course my brother and I first lived at 429 Roe Street.

William Barbour, Manchester Township's attorney when Haledon was incorporated, also was so honored.

When our family left Roe Street in 1948, we moved to Barbour Street.

Tilt Street is named after the largest silk mill owner in town, and John Ryle Avenue commemorates John Ryle, founder of the US silk industry.

In 1913 Haledon became well known for one of the epic labor struggles in American history. Workers in Paterson's mills called a strike because weavers were being asked to operate four looms instead of two. They knew half the people would be let go. In addition, they wanted a twelve-dollar weekly wage, an eight-hour workday instead of ten, and an end to child labor. When these demands were not met, twenty-five thousand workers walked off their jobs, closing three hundred mills and dye houses.

The workers met in halls in Paterson, but many were arrested and declared agitators. The authorities attempted to halt the strike by forbidding employees to hold public meetings anywhere. After the strike ended federal investigators discovered the Paterson police, staffed mainly by Irish Americans, were allied with the manufacturers. Jails overflowed with arrested workers.

Haledon Mayor William Bruekman, a German Socialist, gave the workers a safe haven in his town. Paterson police officers couldn't follow the workers into Haledon.

Pietro and Maria Botto, who emigrated from Biella, a town in the Piedmonte region of Northern Italy, worked in the Cedar Cliff silk mills in Haledon, as did their three daughters. The Botto House on Norwood

Courtesy of American Labor Museum / Botto House National Landmark
Botto House.

Street was offered as an amphitheater for labor leaders to address the thousands of workers who gathered. Many people sat in trees to listen. The house, situated on a hill, had an upper porch overlooking a green field — an excellent platform from which to address the workers below. The area, shaped like a huge bowl, had wonderful natural acoustics.

Leaders of the Industrial Workers of the World (IWW), nicknamed "Wobblies," came to town to support the movement. They recently had settled a textile strike in Lawrence, Massachusetts and rushed down their most capable leaders.

The strike lasted almost six months. As their bills piled up, workers were forced to return to their jobs.

Courtesy of American Labor Museum / Botto House National Landmark
Botto yard with striking workers.

Conditions didn't improve right away but issues such as minimum pay, the eight-hour workday, and change in child labor laws did come to pass.

And so Haledon became famous as a haven of free speech. Labor historians consider the strike a successful struggle for basic bread-and-butter labor needs. In 1983 the Botto family home became the first Italian-American site to be designated a national historic landmark.

Soon after, our ancestors—both the Carnevale and Finamore families—would arrive and help live out the next chapter in the borough's history.

Chapter 2
The Finamores, Our Father's Family

Grandfather Nicola "Nicholas" Finamore migrated to Philadelphia, Pennsylvania first in 1908. Why Philadelphia? We're not certain. Many other Frainese probably had settled there. Grandmother Letizia "Elizabeth" Finamore (nee Marino) said a woman in Italy told her to go to America soon because he might find another woman. At least that's what she told Cousin Joan Alesso (nee Melone).

So Grandma made the ship crossing with their three children—Uncle Pete, the oldest; Aunt Anna Rachele; and Aunt Regina "Jennie." They arrived in America in November 1910 and also went to Philadelphia, where our father was born in 1913.

Finamore family photo

The Finamore family, circa 1927. Left to right: Uncle Pete, Grandfather "Nicholas" Nicola, Aunt Anna Rachael, Father Nick, Aunt "Jennie" Regina, Grandmother "Elizabeth" Letizia.

Now, here's some background on the Finamores, starting with the surname itself. It's a compound of *fina*, which means "fine," and *amore*, or "love." Consider "fine" to be an adjective and the name translates to "fine love." Over the years we've had a difficult time with how people pronounce our name. Many say, "Oh, you mean like James Fenimore Cooper, the American writer." "No," we reply. "It's 'F' as in Frank — F-i-n-a-m-o-r-e." Also, many mistakenly associated the name with Irish ethnicity.

Now, more about Fraine, Italy, the medieval town to which the family traces its origins. It's in the Province of Chieti, Abruzzo in Southern Italy near the Adriatic Sea. Fraine sits on a hill between the Treste

River and the Lama River, against the background of the Apennine Mountains. Atop the hill is a church with a bell tower.

All around the village are houses, separated by narrow alleys and flights of stairs. When my father's parents lived there, its population was about eight hundred.

Virgin Mary Appears

The family told us a fascinating story about an apparition of the Virgin Mary, Mater Domini, that appeared in Fraine in the year AD 1000. In those days the village was in Old Fraine atop the hill. We were given only a brief outline of what happened so we researched for more details. We learned Mary appeared to a poor deaf-mute girl who helped her parents by grazing their herd from dawn to sunset:

One day, while she was sitting alone, with her watchful eyes on the flock, she was hit by a great glow from a large oak tree and heard a strange voice … It was the first time she perceived a sound, and she was stunned and frightened. On the oak tree was a beautiful Lady, dressed in white with a baby in her arms. The Virgin invited her to call her parents. Meanwhile, the parents, busy in their work, hearing her cries, did not respond because they didn't think such sounds could come from their deaf daughter. Confused and resentful at her parents' indifference, the girl returned to the beautiful Lady. The Virgin, encouraging her, replied, "Do not despair. Go back to them and ask them to come here as I have a message for them." The shepherdess again walked over to her parents and called them. They marveled, barely recognizing their daughter, and followed her.

Arriving under the big oak tree, they turned their eyes upward and saw the beautiful Lady. "I am Mary, the Mother of the Lord!" she revealed. "Go to the parish priest of Fraine, show the child, and tell him to build here, to my will, a church, where devotees can come to pray and honor my son." The parents and the girl told the priest what had happened. And from this tale under those same trees in an atmosphere of peace and tranquility, the Sanctuary of Santa Maria Mater Domini was built.[2]

Except for Jesus appearing to the apostles after his death, this apparition is the earliest in church history. Interestingly, though, Our Lady had a similar message at a number of other sites. In Lourdes in 1858, she said, "Go, tell the priest that people should come here in procession and to build a chapel here." And in Fatima in 1917, she said, "I want to tell you that a chapel is to be built here in my honor."

We were told the Fraine apparition didn't become as famous as the others because the townspeople didn't want to be overrun by tourists.

In this place our Grandfather Nicola initially worked as a silk twister on a device invented by Leonardo da Vinci. He twisted silk threads, making them strong enough for the looms. He and the whole family brought their skills to the US where our uncles

Family photo permission of Nicola Finamore and family

Town of Fraine, Italy.

and aunts worked as dyers, spinners, and finishers in Paterson's silk mills. Some performed a "picking" operation; they inspected the woven silk, using a tweezer-like tool to remove knots and loose ends.

In 1936 Nicola and Letizia moved to 66 North Seventh Street, Paterson, just across the Haledon border—the same neighborhood where my mother, Teresa Carnevale, lived. Grandfather Finamore lost a leg to diabetes. When doctors concluded they had to take the other one, too, he refused. Soon after, in 1941, he passed away at age fifty-nine. I was two then, so I never knew him.

At that point Grandma Finamore moved to Morrissee Avenue in Haledon, which was near us after we moved to Barbour Street. She lived with her daughter, our Aunt Anna, who was married to Charles

Melone, and her sister, Aunt Jennie, a spinster. The Melones had two children, Joan and Charles Jr., nicknamed "Junior," which is what we always called him. Joan and Junior were both much older than us.

Uncle Pete lived elsewhere in New Jersey with his spouse and their two sons, Ray and Peter, nicknamed "Whitey."

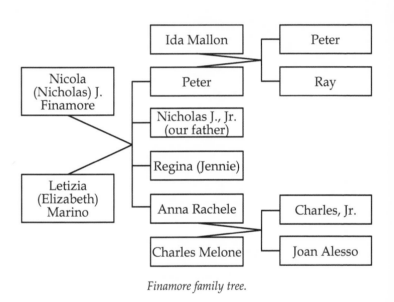

Finamore family tree.

Proverbial Italian Grandma

We remember Grandma Finamore fondly. Our cousin Ray Finamore helped us describe her since he visited her often and became close to her.

"She was the proverbial Italian grandma. She was always dressed in black to mourn our grandfather, who died many years prior to her passing," Ray said, "She had her hair in a bun and wore a black dress, black stockings, and shoes. She carried a black change purse in the pocket of the dress and always called us over to her, squeezed our cheeks, and kissed us all over our faces, saying something in Italian."

"*Vieni qui* (Come here)," she'd say before she opened her purse and handed us some change—a quarter or, on a good day, a fifty-cent piece. We couldn't communicate much because she spoke Italian and only a little English.

Grandma Finamore was a kind, loving person and very hard working. She wore the same black ensemble for Sunday dinners in the basement. Only she added a full-length apron for cooking. She stood on a midsize step stool/ladder, stirring the gravy. That same stool came to be her final step in life.

In January 1960, at eighty, she used the stool to reach for something high in the cabinet. Sadly, she fell, broke her hip, and died of pneumonia while recovering.

Grandma Finamore was a very good cook. She had a way of disguising foods we didn't like. She cooked string beans with potatoes but mixed the combination with red gravy. What kid likes spinach? She crushed spinach and mixed it with mashed potatoes.

My favorite was her escarole and beans—in Italian, *scarola* and beans. For some reason she used canned Campbell's Pork and Beans, turning it into a creamy, delicious concoction. We still make it that way today! (See "Family Recipes" section.)

We often joined the Melone family and Grandma Finamore for dinners, usually without our parents, who were working in their diner. Grandma helped our parents out. Many a day she was at our sink with a washboard (a corrugated galvanized metal board), washing our clothes. In those days there were no washing machines.

She was always concerned about doing for others and never about herself. If we had to describe our Grandma Finamore in a word, it would be "love."

Chapter 3
The Carnevales, Our Mother's Family

O ur maternal grandfather Alphonse Carnevale and grandmother Ester Carnevale (nee Calvano) both immigrated to America from Caserta, a small town in Southern Italy, twenty-one miles north of Naples.

Caserta—its name means "impregnable house"—sits at the base of the Apennine Mountains to the east and stretches to Campania and the sea to the west. Orchards, vineyards, and olive trees embellish the landscape. In 1789 Bourbon King Ferdinando IV founded the Monumental Complex of Belvedere di San Leucio there. This experimental model town was built on land originally purchased as a royal summer retreat and hunting grounds. The king's vision was to create a utopia comprising a silk factory, workers' housing, a school, and indoor and outdoor communal spaces. The complex included the Royal Palace of Caserta, the main residence of the Bourbon kings of Sicily and Naples. At twelve hundred rooms, it rivaled even Versailles in France.

A large community of silk weavers moved into this industrial town, known as the Silk Weavers Royal Colony. The foresighted Code of Law back then guaranteed that male and female workers would enjoy equal rights and salaries, according to their merits. Education was free. The king even gifted a loom to every family in the colony so silk weaving skills would continue through the next generations. Local people were involved in every step of silk production — farming silkworms, twisting threads to make them strong enough for the looms, spinning, dyeing the skeins, weaving on sophisticated looms, and finishing.

In Caserta, a place with such a rich history, our grandfather became a silk weaver. Working alone, he operated a loom with a Jacquard attachment, which held the horizontal silk threads, known as a warp, under tension while vertical threads were interwoven, creating silk cloth. The Jacquard attachment automated how patterns were woven.

Grandfather Carnevale brought his occupation to Paterson, New Jersey, where our mother, Teresa Finamore (nee Carnevale), was born on November 14, 1914.

Moving from Caserta to Paterson, the "Silk City" of the United States, probably was a logical, easy decision for our Carnevale grandparents. The silk manufac-

Courtesy of American Labor Museum / Botto House National Landmark
Silk loom with a Jacquard attachment.

turing companies of Paterson offered work opportunities to a multitude of arriving immigrants. The powerful water flowing from Paterson's Great Falls provided enough electrical energy to support more than three hundred silk mills.

Spanish Flu Tragedy

A few years after our mother was born, trauma struck her life dramatically. She was three when the Spanish Flu Pandemic overtook the world in 1917 and 1918, taking the lives of 20–50 million people. Along with all the other family members, Teresa's mother, Ester, contracted the flu. She refused to follow doctor's orders and get bed rest. Instead she took care of others. Consequently, she died of the illness, leaving Grandfather Alphonse Carnevale to take care of a very young Teresa and her even younger brother, Thomas.

In 1920 Grandfather Carnevale remarried. His new wife was Angelina Deluca. They had two sons, Frank and Alphonse Jr. Young as she was, our mother had to help out at home, even with raising the two baby boys. There wasn't much time or attention left for her, which was probably why she overprotected her own children.

Though our mother, Teresa, was conversant in the Italian language, she didn't teach us because, as was true of many first-generation Italians then, she wanted us to be fully assimilated into America. Later in life, she also went by the nicknames Theresa and Terri.

In 1923 conditions in his homeland would further impact my Grandfather Carnevale's life. That year

Grandpa Carnevale with his first wife, Ester.

Franco Scalamandre of Caserta grew disgusted with the rise of fascism in Italy. A year earlier Benito Mussolini had become prime minister. Increasingly, Italians conceded control of their personal lives to the state. All political and intellectual dissent was suppressed. Like the Nazi Gestapo, the Italian

Finamore family photo

Grandpa Carnevale with his second wife, Angelina.

Blackshirts ruled with an iron hand and made people conform. So-called "troublemakers" were tied to a tree, forced to drink a pint or two of castor oil, or forced to eat a live frog. No wonder Scalamandre fled Italy for a better life in America.

Finamore family photo

Our mother, Teresa Carnevale (standing), with her brothers (left to right) Frank, Alphonse Jr, and Thomas.

One day Scalamandre saw a truckload of looms headed for the dump. He offered the driver, who he didn't know, ten dollars for the load. The driver jumped down.

The Carnevale family, 1952. Left to right: Uncle Al, Mom, Grandmother Angelina, Grandfather Alphonso, Uncle Frank.

"You can't take them without me," he said, "I'm the weaver."

After Scalamandre set up shop in Paterson, he hired Grandpa as a weaver. Grandpa and Grandma Carnevale lived on North Seventh Street in Paterson just on the border of Haledon. He took the trolley to work in Paterson.

In 1929 Scalamandre Silks moved ten looms to an old red brick factory with large green doors in Queens, New York. Grandpa Carnevale stayed with his job, spending many hours each day traveling between Paterson and Queens. His grueling daily commute began with a ride on the Susquehanna (or "Susie-Q")

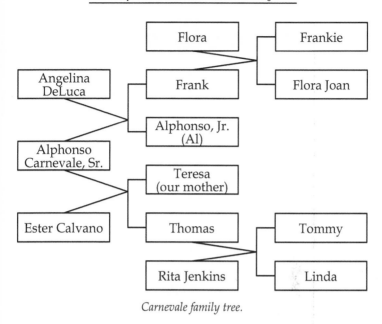

```
        Flora ─────────┐  ┌──── Frankie
                        \ /
Angelina ─┐   Frank ────/ \──── Flora Joan
DeLuca    ├─
          │   Alphonso, Jr.
          │      (Al)
Alphonso ─┘
Carnevale, Sr.  Teresa
          ┌─   (our mother)
Ester     ├─
Calvano   └─   Thomas ────┐  ┌──── Tommy
                           \ /
             Rita Jenkins ──/ \──── Linda
```

Carnevale family tree.

Railroad that would take him as far as the Hudson River; connections from there would eventually get him to Queens. In the evening, he reversed the process.

Our father liked to tell us stories of the severe hardship in those days. A lot of the economic hard times were due to the Great Depression years, starting in 1929 and lasting a decade. Many people were out of work and at times didn't have enough to eat.

Some roads surrounding North Seventh Street were steep hills, our father recalled. To ski down them, he and his friends tied barrel staves to their feet. He also spoke of walking to school for miles in waist-deep snow — a famous story told by many senior citizens who grew up in that decade.

Our father also told us about the most difficult jobs he took to make ends meet. He shoveled cow and horse manure at Buck Gaiz's farm and carried heavy blocks of ice up three flights of stairs for people with iceboxes. Refrigerators didn't go on the market until 1927.

Dye House Sweatshops

Like many residents in the late 1920s, both my parents went to work. Our mother was very upset she could not attend high school. Instead she had to work immediately after graduating grammar school. And when she received her paycheck, it went directly to her parents. Hard times prevailed. (All her life our mother believed in education. She always told us how important it was to get through high school and go on to college.)

She and our father worked in the Haledon silk dye houses, considered sweatshops because the rooms were filled with steam and fumes. Skeins of silk thread were dipped in large vats of hot water and chemicals. My parents told us the dye houses had the dirtiest, unhealthiest jobs in the silk industry.

In 1933 our Carnevale grandparents moved to Twenty-Ninth Street in Astoria, Queens to be closer to Grandpa's work at 37-24 Twenty-Fourth Street. The commute from New Jersey was just too long. Both their sons, our Uncle Frank and Uncle Al, lived with them.

Uncle Frank became a high-level manager at Scalamandre Silks over the course of some years.

Although Uncle Al lived at home, he was a full-time accordion player who traveled for gigs — Florida in the winter and Atlantic City in the summer. I came along six years after the Carnevales moved to Queens. Uncle Al was my music idol from the start! He influenced me so much, I started taking accordion lessons at age seven.

In New York one of the first jobs Grandpa Carnevale worked on was for William Randolph Hearst. He wove six yards of silk fabric for the publishing magnate's stately home.

Eighty percent of Scalamandre Silks production in the 1940s was dedicated to the war effort. They wove fabrics for parachutes and linings for combat helmets and camouflage nets. They also did the weave for the Metropolitan Opera curtain.

As a high-end silk fabrics manufacturer, Scalamandre also produced stock and custom woven textiles for every administration since President Herbert Hoover, including Richard Nixon, Jimmy Carter, Ronald Reagan, Bill Clinton, and both Bushes.

Scalamandre received its highest profile White House commission during the Kennedy Administration. Grandpa Carnevale was on the team that reproduced silk textiles for the Blue Room draperies and the Red Room walls, draperies, and upholstery, all under the guidance of First Lady Jacqueline Kennedy. Their involvement was not publicized because Mrs. Kennedy feared the press would lambast her for such lavishness. Similarly, Franco Scalamandre thought that being associated with her extravagance would hurt his business.

Chapter 4
The Haledon We Knew

No matter who you were, you felt part of the community in Haledon despite ethnic, religious, or political differences. You were a big fish in a small town. Growing up, we got to meet many, if not all, of the five thousand residents at one time or another. As youths, we didn't call adults by their first names. We said "Miss," "Missus," or "Mister."

Now, as was true back in the day, the town is considered low density with mostly detached houses for middle-class, blue-collar workers. A small amount of light industry remains in facilities left over from the silk era boom. Most of Haledon, though, has sprawling greenery and a family-oriented atmosphere. The Molly Ann Brook runs through town. There's forest acreage in two distinct areas as well as a large athletic field on Roe Street.

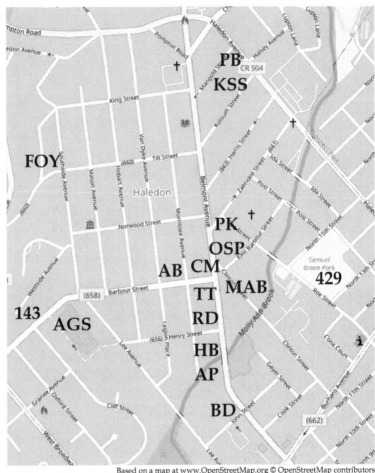

Based on a map at www.OpenStreetMap.org © OpenStreetMap contributors

Our Haledon landmarks.

143 – 143 Barbour St.
429 – 429 Roe St.
AB – Andolino's Barber Shop
AGS – Absalom Grundy School
AP – A&P
BD – Belmont Diner
CM – Coral's Market
FOY – Fountain of Youth

HB – Haledon Bank
KSS – Kossuth Street School
MAB – Molly Ann Brook
OSP – Orapallo Shoe Parlor
PB – Piccininno Barber Shop
PK – Poultry Kill
RD – Romano's Deli
TT – Tony's Tavern

Courtesy of American Labor Museum / Botto House National Landmark
Haledon's "Fountain of Youth."

Haledon is so small, we could walk from one end to the other in less than fifteen minutes. Yet it has its landmarks.

If we got thirsty during the day when we were kids, for instance, we walked or biked to our town's famous "Fountain of Youth," located up the hill on the corner of Southside Avenue and Tilt Street. The fountain was featured in many newspaper articles.

Originally, the water had come up from a clay pipe in the ground. Later they built a horseshoe-shaped stone structure with steps leading down to the pipe outlet. People came from far and wide to get some delicious water, which flowed constantly. Authorities regularly checked for contamination. Many times they closed down access until the water was clear and drinkable again.

Courtesy of American Labor Museum / Botto House National Landmark
Pipe outlet at the Haledon fountatin.

Often there were long lines. Over time nearby neighbors became annoyed with the noise as well as the glass left behind when people broke gallon jugs. They complained. To address these concerns, the spring was moved across the street, an ultraviolet filter was installed, and visiting hours were limited. A sign that read "Haledon Residents Only" was posted. Only town residents got a special key for access.

When Grandma Carnevale moved to Haledon later in life, she brought a large number of glass gallon jugs to the site and filled them. She used the water for drinking, coffee, pasta — everything except bathing. She and our mother both lived to 102. Pure coincidence?

Special Places

Another popular landmark attracted picnickers — Indian Rock, a very large boulder shaped like an Indian chief with a headdress. Upwards of ten people could sit on top.

Above Haledon is High Mountain, offering views to distant New York City. At its peak is Ailsa Farms, dating to 1877. The property and forty-room mansion

Courtesy of American Labor Museum / Botto House National Landmark
Ten people sitting on Indian Rock.

was owned by the family of Garret Hobart, the twenty-fourth US vice president. Hobart served under President William McKinley from 1897 until he died in 1899. In the late nineteenth century dignitaries and prominent businesspeople gathered in the mansion, nestled in a hollow at the estate's southeastern end. The state of New Jersey bought Ailsa Farm in 1948. It's now on the William Paterson University campus.

Haledon is nestled amongst four very unique municipalities — Wayne, famous for its many uninhabited farmlands, to the west; Prospect Park, once a dry town, to the east; Paterson, to the south; and bucolic North Haledon, to the north. They each have special places of their own, too.

During my boyhood I loved going to Murchio Airport in Wayne. It featured a turf runway and biplane rides; the nearby Airport Inn had a life-size plane on the roof and served gigantic hot dogs in its restaurant. I peddled my bike many miles on the Hamburg Turnpike just to watch the planes take off and land. I now realize how dangerous it was to bicycle on a major highway. Though I never told my parents, I dreamed I could get enough money to pay for a plane ride, even without their permission. My flying infatuation probably had a lot to do with the *Sky King* radio broadcast adventure.

Wayne also had the Hinchman Swimming Hole and the Old Barn Milk Bar (Alderney Milk Barn), which served triple-scoop ice cream cones.

Haledon is about one mile from Paterson's Great Falls, a national landmark and the second largest waterfall in volume east of the Mississippi. (The largest is Niagara Falls.) The Great Falls, which drops some seventy-seven feet, once provided the electrical power for the major industries in the city, including Colt gun manufacturing, three locomotive manufacturing plants, and, of course, hundreds of silk mills. About 121 firms were involved in every stage of silk production. John Ryle produced the first skein of silk there and the Jacquard loom was brought in the early 1870s.[3]

Courtesy of American Labor Museum / Botto House National Landmark
Paterson Great Falls.

North Haledon has the picturesque Buttermilk Falls in the High Mountain Preserve, a wooded area we visited frequently with our boyhood friends. It has a straight drop of fifty feet into a manmade canyon, an old sandstone quarry. It, too, was transferred to William Paterson University.

'Peyton Place'

Our mother called Haledon "Peyton Place," after a 1957 movie about residents of a small New England town with a seemingly tranquil façade. There were many sleepy towns like that in America during the post-war years, but they were deceptively quiet. Our mother thought the secret scandals and moral hypocrisy in Haledon mimicked the salacious secrets in *Peyton Place*.

Rumors of love triangles, family feuds, marriage infidelity, jealousy, and sexual secrets were abundant in our one-square-mile town. As the saying goes, "Everyone in town knew one another's business." That's just the way it was: You knew everyone and everyone knew you. So if you caused trouble, word got to your parents before you had an opportunity to inform them.

However, when it came to hardship or loss, the town always pitched in and helped one another.

My Long Recovery

When I was five and still living at Roe Street, I developed hives all over my body. My mother took me to a doctor, who diagnosed a case of poison oak. Because of her past family trauma and experiences, my mother was very caring, particularly with her two children. She disputed the doctor's diagnosis and took me to Dr. Wolf, a pediatric physician in Paterson, who immediately diagnosed rheumatic fever, a staph infection of the heart. He recommended full bed rest for two months in the summertime. Since there was no air conditioning except the screens in open windows, I lay in bed for hours at a time, listening to the kids playing outside. I felt fine and wanted to join them, but I followed my mother's orders. She kept me occupied with many activities, including coloring books, puzzles, books, and toys, but my favorite pastime was listening to serial radio programs.

It's been said that radio, as an invisible medium, has the greatest effect in stimulating the imagination. Here's a rundown of some programs that had dramatic influence in my young life and future choices:

Sky King, a hybrid cowboy/aviation adventure show, featured Schuyler "Sky" King, an Arizona rancher and aircraft pilot. King always captured criminals and sometimes spies. He also found lost hikers using the Songbird, his personal plane. King was a rancher with a deep tone of voice, that is, very upstanding and serious. The intrigue and excitement of *Sky King* probably led me to want

Boyd Magers, Westen Clippings,
www.westernclippings.com
Sky King.

to be a pilot. Later in life, I obtained private, instrument and commercial licenses and became a partner in a four-place Piper Arrow N1554X.

The Green Hornet was a superhero like Superman and Batman. During his travels in the Far East, he saved the life of Kato, who became a loyal friend. Kato's ethnicity throughout the show's run was ambiguously Asian, ranging from Japanese to Filipino to Korean to Chinese.

Gang Busters was an American dramatic radio program heralded as "the only national program that brings you authentic police case histories." Each episode began with a barrage of loud sound effects, including guns firing and tires squealing, leading to the popular catch phrase "came on like gangbusters."

The Shadow serial radio show was based on a character who had "the power to cloud men's minds so they could not see him." The very famous introduction has endured for a place in American lore: "Who knows what evil lurks in the hearts of men? The Shadow knows!" These words were accompanied by an ominous laugh and a musical theme.

Other serial radio programs I enjoyed included the *Lone Ranger, Superman, Batman, Fibber McGee and Molly,* and *Amos 'n' Andy.*

My other main interest during my long recovery was comic books, which were more than just "looking at pictures," as many believed. That's what I initially did at age five, but over time I focused on the characters and plots and had the reading skills to understand the stories more fully. Like baseball cards and toy soldiers, comics were collectibles. Though their initial cost was ten cents, over time their value increased exponentially. We never stored ours long enough for them to accrue value.

I gravitated to other superheroes such as Mighty Mouse, Flash Gordon, and Popeye. I also liked Heckle and Jeckle, Dick Tracy, Li'l Abner, Tom and Jerry, and many others.

I recovered over the two summer months and later had medical checkups that indicated my heart suffered no permanent damage. The care of the doctor and my mother had worked!

Chapter 5
Shopping Back in the Day

Belmont Avenue, West Broadway, and Haledon Avenue were the town's main thoroughfares. They ran north and south. There were no malls in 1940s and 1950s. You found whatever you needed on those streets—bakeries, butcher shops, jewelry stores, drugstores, taverns, diners, barbers, gas stations, post office, laundromats, dry cleaners, shoemakers, dentists, doctors, banks, bowling alleys, photographer, lawyers, restaurants, and even a hotel.

Most stores were close enough to walk to. Everyone in town knew each other and frequented one another's businesses.

When we meandered on the sidewalks and stopped in various shops, we inevitably met a neighbor, family member, or friend and spent some time catching up on the latest rumors and news. As young children, though, we were antsy and just wanted to move on, so we bugged our mother to stop the chitchat.

We'll take you on a stroll up and down Haledon's streets of commerce.

Haledon's Barber Shops

Visiting the barbershop with our father was a great tradition. We went to the same barbers — Lou Piccininno's on Haledon Avenue or Tony Andolino's on Barbour Street, both sole proprietors, for most of our life. Andolino had another barber named Casey who cut hair so they had two chairs operating most times. It was there we overheard the older men discussing news of the day, "Peyton Place" Haledon rumors, and other town gossip. There were also conversations about cars, sports, politics, and family life. Even as a young child, I sensed the barbershop was a fun hangout for men.

Occasionally, jokes were told. My first exposure to swear words and dirty jokes was in the barbershop, though I didn't fully understand them all. Everyone got involved — the barbers with interesting stories to tell, the customers getting their hair cut, and those waiting their turn as they read newspapers and magazines. Haircuts were an enjoyable experience because all of us, young, old and middle-aged, joined the debates and conversation.

When we entered either shop, we immediately smelled the scents and aromas of hair tonic, pomades, oils, and neck powder. I was fascinated with all the barber stuff — the razors, scissors, even the long leather strap that hung from the arm of the chair. The barbers used that strap to hone their razors to their target sharpness. The chair wasn't much different from today's. It had head and leg rests. A hand-operated handle was used to raise or lower the chair to accommodate the customer's height. The chair also rotated and could lean backwards. The ones at Piccininno's and Andolino's were made of cast iron with leather. They appeared very expensive and heavy.

Outside both shops were red, white, and blue poles with spiraling stripes. We researched the history of those poles and discovered they were symbols from olden times, up to the 1500s, when barbers performed medical procedures. The stripes represented bandages, blood, and blue veins. I'm glad we missed those days.

The Poultry Kill

Our mother walked us to the fresh live poultry store on Belmont Avenue, either Giardino's or Bredder's Poultry. Bob and I liked to observe the processing of a fresh hen. As I walked in, my senses were filled with smells and sounds foreign to me. The smell was bearable. The sound was a very loud cacophony of squawks from white-feathered chickens sitting in cages, waiting to be slaughtered. A man in a dirty apron, heavy black boots, and gloves walked over to my mother.

"What size?" he asked.

"Not that one," my mother often replied, "the one over there."

After the bird was chosen, picked up by its legs, and removed from the cage, it was weighed as its head dangled down. It was then taken into a back room where, as we watched, a cleaver chopped down on a large butcher block, decapitating it. We saw the cuts. There were hundreds of lines in the hardwood.

After its blood was drained into a large vat, the chicken was thrown into a hot water tank to loosen its feathers. The man plucked off all the feathers, wrapped the carcass in wax paper, and handed it to us. The process was quite something for a youngster to witness. But even as young tykes, we accepted the way chickens were killed without horror. To us, it was a way of life, what needed to be done. Besides, we had fresh chicken for dinner!

The Tavern Piano Roll

When I was ten my father took me to Tony's Tavern near the corner of Barbour and Belmont. I don't know if the laws in those days allowed a minor in the establishment, but there I was. My father didn't drink at all. For him Tony's was an opportunity to mingle with his close Haledon friends.

As I entered a tavern for the first time, I noticed the different-colored liquor bottles behind the long bar, which curved into the dimly lit large room. A number of oak tables were scattered around. Patrons sat on stools facing the bar as the bartender drew drafts of beer and poured drinks. The conversation and laughter were loud. In those days there were a lot of smokers so the room was dense with a thick fog. My father smoked one pack of non-filter Pall Malls per day though he gave them up later in life.

What drew my attention most was a large upright piano against one wall. It played itself as a paper roll with punch holes was pulled over a metal bar. Mesmerized, I stood in front of it for a very long time, watching the keys get depressed as the song played. The bartender came over and told me that George Gershwin, the prolific songwriter who wrote "Rhapsody in Blue" and many other favorites in the Great American Songbook, learned to play piano as a young boy by placing his fingers in the depressed keys of a player piano.

Not certain if the story was true, I did some research and discovered it was. As an adult, Gershwin recorded piano rolls between 1916 and 1927 to earn extra money. That afternoon left a lasting impression on me. The memory, together with my music training, influenced me to buy a Yamaha Disklavier player piano in 2017. It uses digital electronics instead of paper rolls, which employed a pneumatic mechanism to depress the keys. What a joy to purchase the Yamaha! It has provided many hours of live piano music, which I can control with an app on my cell phone or laptop computer.

I even tried Gershwin's method and followed the depressed keys on a solo jazz piano arrangement I wanted to learn. It worked!

Shoe Parlor

Bob: Another store we liked was Orapallo's Shoe Repair Shop on Belmont Avenue. Mr. Orapallo, the sole proprietor, usually was the only worker we saw. He advertised "Shoe Repair While You Wait." As we entered his store, we smelled the distinct fresh odor of leather and dyes. We watched as Mr. Orapallo removed a worn sole or heel from a shoe and made a rough surface so a new one would stay in place. He then chose a ready-made replacement or cut one from a new piece of leather.

Next came attaching the replacement with nails, cement, or stitching and then trimming the part to fit by buffing it on a large lathe turning machine. At the same time he buffed and stained to match the color of the shoe. The process, fascinating to watch while you wait, is rare to find these days.

Italian Deli

We frequently shopped for Italian food at Romano's Italian Delicatessen at 301 Belmont Avenue. When I walked in with my mother, I instantly salivated at the sight of so many mouth-watering wonders. The deli case was loaded with traditional antipasto ingredients and a range of cheeses. I savored the pungent aroma of sharp provolone, which smelled like moldy gym socks left out in the rain. There were slabs of imported prosciutto, mortadella, and soppressata (Italian dry salami). Loaves of crusty Italian bread were stacked on shelves. And there was enough broccoli rabe, olives, and garlic to ward off a family of vampires.

The floors were dark oak and there were rather large front picture windows for viewing into the store.

Mr. Romano Jacob, the owner, was from Piedmont, a region in northern Italy near Milan, bordering France and Switzerland. He spoke Italian with my mother, but there were occasions the dialect was so different from my mother's Southern Italian speech, they had a difficult time understanding each other. So they both defaulted to English for the remaining conversation.

I fondly recall my mother complaining that he cut the cold cuts too thin. Every time! He never cut them to her satisfaction. The weight was the same in the end, as was the price, but for some unknown reason, he had the slicing machine set to a thin cut.

Leo Wallerius owned the pork and butcher shop next store at 303 Belmont, where we bought some of our pork. I attended elementary school with his daughter, Doris.

Coral's Market

Bob: The story of Americo and Elise Coral was typical of many immigrant families who sought the "American Dream." Americo's father, who emigrated from Piedmont, changed the family name from Corallo to Coral to avoid the anti-Italian prejudice they felt in those days.

Americo, born in America a year after his father came to this country, became a butcher. He married Elise, who was of Swiss ancestry, and eventually settled in Haledon. The couple rented a store and an apartment above it. They had three children, Louis, Arthur, and Barbara, all born there.

Arthur, the younger brother, was known as Itchy. Older brother Lou told us Arthur had contracted poison ivy in the location of his groin when he was very young. Like most kids, he scratched the area, which brought temporary relief. In Arthur's case, the scratching was temporary but the nickname Itchy stuck his whole life.

The boys' sister Barbara was nicknamed Mousey. Not even Lou could explain how she got that name. It's a lasting mystery!

Coral's Market was centrally located in the very busy Belmont Avenue business district on the corner of Barbour Street. The entire family worked hard to make it a success. They employed as many as seven other people to handle various tasks, too. At the time the larger supermarkets—A&P, ACME, Kroger,

Safeway — were not in the area. Coral's was the town supermarket until A&P eventually built a store one block away, alongside Molly Ann Brook on Belmont Avenue.

Prior to the A&P, though, we took a short walk from our home, down Barbour Street, to Coral's Market, where we would purchase most of the meat, fruits, vegetables, canned goods, and deli items we needed. They had it all. The business continued for fifty years.

During the 1950s Lou and Itchy went into the newspaper delivery business. They bought a van that you drove standing up. It had sliding doors that opened on both sides so they could toss the morning paper, the Morning Call, and the evening paper, the Paterson Evening News, to homes and businesses in Haledon, Prospect Park, and Paterson. "Coral Brothers" was painted on the sides. They delivered to mailboxes, front porches, driveways, and storefronts.

My brother and I worked for the Coral Brothers' paper delivery service. Lou and Itchy were fun to work for. You had two brothers with very different personalities. Itchy was quiet and low key while Lou was excitable, assertive, and a risk-taker. Itchy was more career-oriented; he went on to college and, upon graduation, joined the corporate world. Lou was more committed to the family business.

Back then we were all delivering papers. Either Lou or Itchy drove. My brother and I, depending on who was working that day, stood in the opposite doorway. While bracing ourselves, we proceeded to

Coral Brothers van.

fold and then toss the papers on lawns, driveways, or porches. (Folding was a unique way to wrap the paper so it could be thrown some distance without unfolding.) If we broke a window, we had to fund the replacement. When the weather was inclement, the newspapers had to be folded and placed into plastic bags before being thrown for delivery.

The Sunday editions were so large and bulky, we wrapped them with elastic bands so they held together. Before we started our route, we were in the grocery store basement slipping lots of advertisement inserts into every issue. They were too big to throw. So there was lots of running on Sundays.

The paper delivery business was a secondary source of income for Itchy and Lou. Nick and I both worked for them at some point as driver or paperboy. We both had interesting and scary situations during our seven-day-a-week careers there.

One day Nick was out with substitute driver Louis Obaytek. At the highest point on King Street, while driving down the steep hill, Louis turned to him.

"Let's try something new," he said. "I will place the truck in second gear. Then both of us will get out and run down the hill, throwing the papers to houses on both sides of the street."

So they ran down in front of the truck for fifty yards, papers in their hands, and then hopped back in. All that time, the truck was unmanned. This system was extremely dangerous. They were fortunate the truck didn't pop out of gear and speed down the hill on its own. As many New York area Italian-Americans like to say, "Fuhgeddaboudit!"

One very cold, icy early morning, I had another memorable experience delivering newspapers, again with substitute driver Louis Obaytek filling in for Lou. We reached a very steep section of the route. Due to treacherous road conditions, Louis was reluctant to drive the truck down the hill. So he walked down the hill to the corner of West Broadway and Katz Avenue and used the pay phone outside the deli to call Lou Coral, who immediately came to our location and jumped into the truck.

Before he proceeded down the hill, he asked us if we wanted to ride with him.

"No thanks!" we both answered.

While we walked down the hill, delivering papers on foot, Lou began his descent. As the truck began to slide, Lou attempted to turn into a homeowner's driveway. Unfortunately, the tires on the driver's side slid into the curb, causing the truck to tip over on its side. Since both doors always remained open, Lou could have been thrown from the vehicle and crushed to death. Realizing the truck was about to flip, though, he wrapped his arms and legs around the steering column in hopes of saving his life. He lived another day to deliver papers!

Another former employee of the Coral Brothers who we got to know is Leo Fracalosy. He moved to California in 1968 and contacted us recently about his many memories of his days living in Haledon.

One of his duties was to go house-to-house to collect the 32¢ weekly charge for delivery of the Paterson Evening News. He told us that when he went to our house at 143 Barbour Street to collect, our mother would give him two quarters and told him to keep the change.

He gave us a great example of the good-hearted and caring nature of the Haledon community. Leo grew up in the neighborhood of Hobart Avenue. His father passed away when he was 5 years old so his mother cleaned houses for a living, and therefore, could not be home to prepare lunch for him and his younger brother Joe. So every weekday they would have lunch at a different neighbor's house. Some of the neighbors included the Gallos, the Caudas, the Rossos and Harry (the plumber) and spouse Adeline Garbaccio. Another neighbor on the block, Rose Rolando, referred to herself as Leo's second mom. She had four children of her own.

It really does take a village.

Morningside Greenhouse

Morningside Greenhouse, owned by the Fisher family for eighty-four years, was one of the oldest businesses in town. Benjamin Fisher made his dream come true after working at the Paterson Rose Company. He opened his own florist shop in North Haledon but then moved to a new building at West Broadway and Central Avenue, just around the block from our address at 143 Barbour Street.

Morningside was a very short walk for us when we wanted spring flowers for a table vase or major occasions, such as birthdays, weddings, or funerals.

Dentistry Revolution

My parents took us to Dr. Coppelman, the local dentist on Belmont Avenue. Inevitably, he found one or more cavities. He looked down my open mouth with a spotlight mounted on a headband. I was scared to death of the pain during any treatment. In those early dentistry days, there was no Novocain to suppress the pain of drilling out a tooth cavity. More than that, the drills they used operated at a much slower speed than those of today. It took forever to drill out the decay.

Dental drills were powered by electric motors mounted several feet away. Rotation was driven by two to three sets of thin belts mounted on wheels. When the dentist used a large drill to remove the decay, you could almost count the rotations; they were long and painful. Ouch!

Later the air-driven, high-speed handpiece revolutionized dentistry. When it was paired with the use of local anesthetic, such as Novocain, trips to the dentist's office became much faster and relatively painless.

When I was a kid, fillings were a dental amalgam — a mixture of metals such as mercury and a powdered alloy of silver and copper. We lived with all that metal in our mouths for years and years until metal was replaced with much safer composite and ceramic materials.

In those days fluoride was not deposited in our drinking water so we developed a lot more tooth cavities than people do today. Fluoride research determined that brown stains on teeth were related to the water supply. Scientists also linked high levels of natural fluoride to fewer cavities so, over a long period, fluoride was introduced into local reservoirs.

Both our parents had to have all their teeth pulled and replaced with dentures. Because of their experience, Bob and I vowed to pay attention to our oral hygiene. Of course, we were aided by technology developments over time—non-shredding dental floss, electronic toothbrushes, X-rays, crown restorations, and new materials. All have allowed us to prevent gum disease and retain most of our teeth.

Home Delivery

We purchased some items directly at home from delivery vehicles. Dugan Brothers, for instance, had trucks that delivered bread and pastry. Other businesses delivered milk, coal, fruits, and vegetables. An individual came to your home, took your knives, and sharpened them in his specially outfitted truck.

Bob: I worked for one of the many individuals who made a living delivering to homes. Norman Gravino, who lived in Haledon, delivered fresh bottled milk to town residents. I woke up at 4:00 a.m. and walked to Norman's house on Central Avenue to begin the delivery route.

He drove his own delivery truck while I stood at the passenger-side doorway. At the rear of the truck were cases of milk loaded in crates and covered with ice. Every customer had an insulated milk case at their side or main entrance door. When we pulled up to a house, we grabbed glass bottles of milk, walked to the home, collected the empties, and deposited the fresh milk in cases. I had a knack for whistling. Norman frequently warned me, "Bob, knock it off. You'll wake the customers!"

Even though the milk cases were insulated, on freezing days the customers occasionally found that frozen cream had risen from the milk and popped the seal off the top of the bottles.

We also got bleach called "no worry" (in Italian slang, *biancoline*) delivered. And then there was the junk man with a horse-pulled open wagon, a unique vehicle in those days. He picked up scrap metal and other miscellaneous throwaway items. He appeared homeless and disheveled but we found out later he was a very rich man.

Also, doctors made house calls when someone had an illness. They came into the house with a small black bag filled with a stethoscope, thermometer, and other medical paraphernalia in order to check vital signs and diagnose diseases and conditions. If a family member came down with a communicable disease, such as chicken pox, measles, or mumps, a red quarantine sticker was placed on the front door to inform visitors to stay away.

Overall, there was little concern about crime. We usually left our windows and doors unlocked since home invasions, carjackings, burglaries, muggings, murders, or assaults were unusual.

Trips to the Big City

If you couldn't find what you needed in Haledon, you hopped on the No. 14 or No. 42 Haledon bus and rode to the large department stores in Paterson, such as Meyer Brothers or Quackenbush. The other major reason to go to Paterson was seeing a first-run movie. There were seven theaters to choose from—The Fabian, The Plaza, The Garden, The Majestic, The US, The Regent, and The Rivoli. The admission price was fifty or seventy-five cents. The attraction before the full feature film usually was part of a science fiction serial, such as the story of *Flash Gordon*, who visited the planet Mongo where he encounters the evil emperor, Ming the Merciless. The story was shown in chapters, week after week for thirteen weeks, to keep people coming back to see what happens next.

The full feature show usually was also preceded by Movietone newsreel clips of current news events and a Looney Tunes cartoon. At the end Porky Pig stuttered, "Th-th-th-that's all folks!" All for fifty cents!

The Plaza Theater on Union Boulevard in nearby Totowa also had "races." You received a number with your purchased ticket. The number corresponded to an individual or vehicle during a race on the screen. If you had the number that won the race, you won a prize.

When we rode the bus to Paterson, we sometimes got off on Main Street in front of Woolworth's, a department store we called the "Five and Dime." Inside were open racks of toy lead soldiers dressed in World War II uniforms and regalia, which we purchased for ten cents apiece. Much like sets of Topps baseball cards, which included several cards and sticks of bubble gum, the soldiers became very valuable as time passed. Unfortunately for us, the toy lead soldiers suffered the same fate as the baseball cards: they were relegated to the disposal bin. Just another small fortune tossed away.

When we were kids the Irish already had populated Paterson to a high degree. Many had become policeman. There was friction between the Italians and the Irish, but since we worked together and had Catholicism as a common bond, the two groups intermarried. Tensions subsided over time.

Chapter 6
The Belmont Diner

D iner historians believe the classic stainless steel diner was a futuristic dream when Walter Scott cut holes for windows in the canvas sides of his horse-drawn wagon in 1872 and rode down Main Street in Providence, Rhode Island. His wagon, stocked with steaming coffee, boiled eggs, sandwiches, and homemade pie, was thought to be the first "night lunch wagon." Late-night workers in factories could get something to eat after the restaurants closed for the evening. The concept evolved into a wheeled "two hot dogs and a cup o' coffee for a nickel" lunch wagon, a comfortable eatery for working-class people.

As electric streetcars replaced the horse-drawn trolley, shabby wagons and retired trolley cars gave way to distinctly permanent walk-in structures along the main streets and highways of the US. Even the smallest was at least twice the length of a standard wagon.

In 1913 Jerry O'Mahony of Bayonne, New Jersey built deluxe Pullman train car look-alikes. Since night lunches no longer provided sufficient income, the new cars expanded to serve breakfast, lunch, and dinner. They were called "dining cars," later cut short to "diners." Many thought the blueprint for diners came from railroad cars, but they evolved into structures all their own. The only connection was the term "diner."[4]

Soon several companies were constructing their own custom-made diners built in factories and transported by train, truck, or ship to their permanent locations.

Enter our father. During World War II he left the silk mills to work for Curtiss-Wright in Paterson. Because the company was involved in government manufacturing of aeronautical parts, he was temporarily protected from the World War II draft.

He'd always wanted to get into business with his brother, Pete. So in 1944 he started the Belmont Diner on Belmont Avenue, one of Haledon's main thoroughfares. Based on what he told us, Dad bought the diner and more than an acre running from Lee Avenue to Belmont Avenue on the border of Molly Ann Brook. He got a great deal in 1944 because the 1920s diner on the property had been abandoned. When the owner went bankrupt, the bank took over the place.

We know the Belmont Diner was built in the late '20s in the Jerry O'Mahony Diner Company's

Drawing by Andrew Jones

Belmont Diner.

Elizabeth, New Jersey manufacturing facility. It was shipped via truck to the Haledon site, and placed by crane on the cinder block foundation. It was the diner company's Victory type, eleven feet wide and thirty feet long, and built with a combination of wood frame and channel iron with sheet metal construction. It had a signature barrel roof with two sheet metal exhaust fan vents on top. The eaves of the roof were open at the end walls.

Inside, the tan-colored marble counter ran the length of the car, making for more seating and food preparation. Along the front of the counter were seventeen swivel and removable stools with white porcelain bases and steel foot rests. The stools were finished with red Naugahyde upholstery. When Bob and I swept and mopped the tile floors, we removed the rotating stools and placed them on the counter. The floor was made of small white octagonal tiles, making it easier to clean.

The kitchen side included a built-in refrigerator, a chopping block sandwich board, deep fryer, gas stove, steam table, NCR cash register, bakery display case, coffee urns, and other standard commercial kitchen appliances. The grill was behind the counter, too, allowing us to continuously talk and interact with our customers.

Much of the back bar was covered with a metal hood containing exhaust fans. The wood menu boards were mounted high on the face for better viewing.

People entered the diner in the center through a sliding front door that had a symmetrical façade of five windows on each side. Two large exhaust fans on the roof provided complete ventilation for the diner interior.

The windows, doors, and original icebox were all manufactured using mahogany with a high-gloss finish. Later we added an adjacent building to the right side to provide restrooms and booths, which women patrons preferred over sitting on a counter stool.

Bob and I found Skee's Diner, an existing vintage O'Mahony diner from the late '20s in Torrington, Connecticut. It's almost identical to our diner. The building, originally situated in Old Saybrook, Connecticut, moved to Torrington in 1944. The Torrington Historic Preservation Trust has embarked on a major project to restore, relocate, and reopen the diner on a site to be determined. The diner closed in

Mark McEachern photo used with permission of the Torrington Historical Society
Skee's Diner, Torrington, Connecticut.

2001. It was placed on the National Register of Historic Places the following year.[567]

Two other diners in town competed with the Belmont—Tier's Diner on Haledon Avenue and the Haledon Diner at the corner of Haledon and Belmont avenues. New Jersey was, and still is, the diner capital of the world.

Our diner was close to both our residences so our dad walked to work, usually leaving at 5:30 a.m. to get ready for the early morning workers starting their days. His first order of business was to get the Red Circle coffee brewing in the two ten-gallon stainless steel gas-fired urns and then set up for the morning breakfast crowd. Many times I walked back home with him at the end of the day, trying to mimic his footsteps. Over time many people have told me, "You walk like your father."

Mark McEachern photo used with permission
of the Torrington Historical Society
Counter at Skee's Diner, Torrington, Connecticut.

Bob: My brother and I started working as short order cooks and cleaners at the early ages of seven and eight. We performed a seemingly structured and rehearsed set of dance moves to prepare some meals. As an example, we opened the big stainless steel metal door to the built-in refrigerator, sitting to the left of the grill. We took out the hamburgers, peeled off the paper, and plopped the patties on the already greased grill. Sizzle! Wait! We flipped them with the spatula. Press. Louder sizzle! Next came the fries blanching in a mesh basket immersed in the deep oil fryer. We twisted the basket and emptied it onto the plate and added garnish with mayo, lettuce, and tomato. Voilà! A complete burger ballet![8]

Similarly, we grilled bacon and eggs, Taylor Ham (pork roll), and Bacon, Lettuce and Tomato sandwiches (BLTs), cut into four triangles.

No mechanical potato peelers in those days. We were given a one hundred-pound bag of Idaho potatoes and a swivel potato peeler. We sat and peeled every potato so our father could slice each one into French fries and prepare them for blanching.

Bob and I also were responsible for filling the glass salt and pepper shakers. We added uncooked grains of rice to the salt so the rice would soak up excess moisture and keep the salt from clumping. We also filled the stainless steel napkin holders with paper napkins.

Although Dad did this most of the time, we occasionally scrubbed the large grill with a pumice stone to remove fried-on food. Residual food was always left over from frying hamburgers, eggs, bacon, and the well-liked Taylor Ham. At the same time we changed the oil in the deep fryer. We placed the leftover grease into five-gallon canisters and saved the congealed residue for the tallow company. Once a week the tallow man came by and gave our dad a nominal fee for the canisters filled with the solidified grease. It was another way to generate income. We understood the grease was later refined and used for making candles.

We also mopped the ceramic tile floors and generally did any menial tasks that came along. The dishes, bowls, mugs, pots, pans, and utensils were all behind and under the counter. The slop sink was there, too, so we could hand-wash all the dirty dishes and utensils. There were no dishwashing machines back then.

We also set up the daily menu on the black felt changeable menu board. There were white alpha and numeric letters with tabs that had to be perfectly placed to spell out the day's menu. We had a box with small compartments containing about three hundred letters, A–Z, and numbers, 1–10, including a dollar sign. There were no printed handout menus. The board hung on the back wall in the middle of the dining car for all patrons to view.

The dress code was simple: We wore white aprons that became grease splattered. Dad wore a starched white shirt and pants and sometimes a white soldier cap, slanted to one side.

We sold a cup of coffee for five cents at the Belmont. Here's what we paid for other items: a loaf of white bread, 10¢; a gallon of milk, 67¢; a dozen eggs, 59¢; a US postage stamp, 3¢; a gallon of gas, 21¢. A new car was $1,125.

Our father made all kinds of homemade soups, including split pea, navy bean, pasta fagioli, chicken noodle, tomato rice, and Manhattan clam chowder. Hardworking people would come in for a bowl of homemade soup and buttered hard roll for 25¢.

Over time Dad developed a secret recipe for homemade hot dog chili sauce, served over mustard and onions on a hot dog within a bun. The deep-fried New Jersey hot dog served this way was famously called a "Texas Weiner." If you wanted yours with the onions, mustard, and chili sauce, you would say, "All the way."

Dad was proud of his formula. After he passed we found his recipe hidden in ten secret places. It called for making ten gallons of sauce at a time, so we adjusted the formula for a suitable family-size portion. We can't share the recipe. If we did, we'd have to shoot you. (See "Family Recipes" section.)

Bob: One of my fond memories was the delivery of pies by Mrs. Smith. The truck driver arrived at the diner with a portable display case and asked my father what he needed. He had a selection of Chocolate Cream, Lemon Meringue, Apple, Blueberry, Coconut Custard, and more. Yummy! The driver placed the pies in our large bakery display case behind the counter. Also on display was the homemade jello and rice pudding my dad made.

Next to the bakery display case was our steam table, referred to as a bain-marie. The gas burners underneath the stainless steel reservoir heated the water, creating steam. Its top had a number of holes to insert pots or long pans. The bain-marie kept pre-cooked soups, meatballs, and other food items at safe food-holding temperatures for dishing out during the day.

Other "droolworthy" dessert treats we kept in the refrigerator included the Charlotte Russe, no longer seen today. It was made from a thin layer of sponge cake topped with a spiral of whipped cream and a Maraschino cherry on top. It was placed in a frilled cardboard holder with a loose round cardboard bottom. You pushed the round cardboard up after eating the whipped cream so you could get at the cake. Charlotte Russe was usually served in upscale restaurants, but we got regular deliveries to the diner.[9]

An Italian dessert prevalent at the time was Biscuit Tortoni—ice cream made with eggs and heavy cream, usually topped with crushed amaretto cookies. It was served in a small paper soufflé cup. A delivery man brought these popular fine desserts, too. To the disappointment of our customers, we often ran out.[10]

Another popular feature was our Coca Cola soda case, filled with odd-flavored sodas, including grape, orange, and pineapple, along with more typical choices—Yoo-hoo, Coke, Dad's Root Beer, Birch Beer, and more. The drinks were submerged in ice and water. We had to reach in and pick out what the customer ordered, momentarily freezing our hand.

A Situation Comedy

Many town residents frequented the diner daily. In the morning the Belmont was a situation comedy. There was the comedian, the satirist, the artistic painter, the botanist, the referee, and the entrepreneur.

We also had the plumber, oilman, body shop man, milkman, mailmen, the Dugan's delivery truck driver, town employees, policemen, A&P employees, and more. It was the town meeting place where people talked politics and news of the day and constantly joked with and harassed one another.

The closeness of the stools at the counter was conducive to one patron joining in others' conversations. Our patrons were so diverse, working the counter was like working at the United Nations. In fact, some customers came in the morning just to listen to the banter. Many customers were combat veterans, while others, including our father, had been drafted near the end of the war and never deployed overseas.

Bob: Joe Garbaccio, the town clerk, was one of those combat veterans. He was so severely wounded during the Normandy Invasion that he lost his right leg and received a Purple Heart. He claimed the Germans and Japanese surrendered because of how fiercely the early Army draftees and enlistees fought.

Meanwhile, my father jokingly argued, "When the Germans and Japanese heard that the married men were entering the war, they decided to surrender."

Another famous story was from Eddie Robertiello, who owned a nearby auto body shop. One day he was eating the Manhattan clam chowder.

"Nick, the string must have broken," he exclaimed. "I found a clam in my soup!" Ha-ha!

Eddie also complained about my father's "famous" meatloaf. He insisted it was the reason for his ulcer.

However, he ordered it every day my father had it on the menu.

Our plumber customer, Harry Garbacio, another Haledon resident, had a helper he called "Primo." Harry shouted his name out very loudly. "Primo!" he'd say. Strange, but as a habit, he called out his wife's name the same way. "Adeline!"

Harry started major debates with an opening question.

"What was the greatest invention ever by man in history?" he asked. Then he answered himself, "It was the toilet."

Then someone in the morning crowd would yell out.

"No, it was the wheel!" Then someone else chimed in.

"No, it was Gutenberg's printing press."

And so the boisterous debate began.

In his younger days, Harry fought in the Diamond Gloves tournament in Paterson and won his bout in the welterweight division. His flat nose reflected the result of many fights.

Harry owned the house across the street from Leo Fracalosy. Leo told us that one summer he had a big job of re-piping the "Old Salt Restaurant" on Route 4 in Paramus. Harry worked on that project for many years and Leo's job was to drop down into the crawl space and dig trenches under all the pipes. It could be 100 degrees down there and there were rats. At the end of the week (on a rainy Friday night), he made the mistake of knocking on Harry's door and asking to get paid. There was a dispute on the amount of pay and they had a fist-fight in front of Harry's house. At the time, Harry was 55 or 60 and Leo was about 15.

Harry, as a former boxer, injured Leo's ribs, but Leo was able to get him on the ground and knock his glasses off so he couldn't see in the rain. Harry's wife Adeline came out of the house yelling at both of them, then running inside and coming out with a glass of water and throwing it on them as they were rolling around in the rain and mud.

The next day they went to work like nothing had ever happened.

We found out Primo was a world-class golf caddie on the PGA tour. One day, during a local golf tournament, he brought in the pro he was caddying for — Roberto De Vicenzo, one of the top golfers in the world. None of us had any idea who he was because we didn't follow golf. He was very insulted no one asked for his autograph. De Vicenzo was from Argentina. In 1967 he beat Jack Nicklaus at the British Open. He was most famous, though, for losing the 1968 Augusta Masters Tournament after he was disqualified on a scoring error: he marked his score card with a "4" instead of the "3" he shot on a par-three hole. According to PGA golfing rules, once he had signed the card, the error could not be changed.

Bob: Another professional golfer he caddied for was Dr. Cary Middlecoff, a former dentist from Memphis, Tennessee. I met him in Memphis when I

was in college playing football for Memphis State University. Dr. Middlecoff was a major sponsor of the university and helped many young football players in the mid-1960s.

Another morning customer told stories about his very enviable job delivering baked goods directly to homes. We called him George "Dugan" because of the sign on the side of the delivery truck he drove: "Dugan's — Bakers for the home since 1878." We never knew his real last name. Dugan picked up the goods from the baking plant in early morning. Then he delivered fresh bread, cupcakes, pastries, potato chips, and other baked items right to people's front door. He had regularly scheduled customers, along with others who placed a large brown-colored "D" in their window so he would stop there.

Dugan often told stories of his escapades with the stay-at-home moms on his routes. He held court as the other customers surrounded him. We could almost hear them whispering to each other as they followed along, "And so — ? And so — ?" I am certain he exaggerated what occurred many times for the delight of his audience. We knew little about what was going on with Dugan's braggadocio at the time, but Bob and I liked the cupcakes he delivered. They each had dark chocolate frosting on top that was a quarter-inch deep. There was nothing like eating the icing on top before getting to the fluffy yellow cake.

Dugan was also a major Yankee baseball fan and claimed to be a good friend of George Herman "Babe" Ruth. We never did confirm it!

Photo Courtesy of DeGolyer Library, Southern Methodist University,
Robert Yarnell Richie Photograph Collection

Dugan's van.

Another notable customer, Otto Charles Benz, was a nationally prominent artistic painter of everyday scenes in North Jersey. A refined gentleman with a frail build, he also was an authority on botany, horticulture, mineralogy, astronomy, and textile design. He was born in Paterson in 1882. When we knew him he was "an old-timer" in his sixties.

We found out later that his paintings, including "Carnival in Haledon" and "High Mountain," were on display in the Smithsonian Institution in Washington, DC, and he was listed in the national *Who's Who in American Art*. Mr. Benz was self-taught. Much of his work is impressionist with bright colors and well-executed sky features. His works today sell from $200 to $650.

One day while walking to school, I saw him standing on the corner of Belmont Avenue and Kossuth Street painting an old house across the street. Each day he stood there with his colored brushes, painting. I was fascinated by how well he captured the scene.

One of Mr. Benz's peculiar luncheon routines was ordering a roast beef sandwich at the diner every single day. He said he needed the protein and iron vitamin associated with red meat because of a medical condition he had. The rumor was that he lived during the Civil War, probably because he was the oldest customer we had at the time.

Many employees of the A&P and the Haledon Bank made the short walk down to the diner on their breaks and lunch hour, even for just a cup of coffee. The Red Circle brand coffee my father used in his large drip urns was freshly ground at the A&P. His customers always raved about his coffee.

Edgar's Antics

Bob: One of my favorite iconic characters was Edgar Cartotto, a customer about eight years older than us who frequented the diner almost daily. His father owned the Cedar Cliff Hotel and Restaurant across the street and further north on Belmont

Avenue—a short walking distance from the diner. Because of our closeness in age, we called him Edgar.

We found out from others that Edgar's mother didn't want him to play sports because of a medical condition. Therefore, he didn't become a very good athlete when he was young. Because his father was wealthy, though, he went to the athletic fields with large bags of baseball gloves, bats, basketballs, footballs, and other sporting equipment and proceeded to referee or umpire the games.

As he matured and developed his skill and talent, Edgar went on to become a famous and respected referee for basketball, working ten NCAA tournaments, fourteen NIT events, the Big East, and the ECAC-Metro/East Coast conference. He also was a baseball coach and umpire who enjoyed an outstanding reputation. While serving as referee, supervisor, and leading rules interpreter, Edgar also was a baseball coach, teacher, and English Department head at Paterson's John F. Kennedy High School. When he was our English teacher earlier at Paterson Central High School, he berated us for calling him Edgar, the only name we knew him by, instead of Mr. Cartotto.

He was known for many outrageous stories. While coaching high school baseball, Edgar once sent a player to the plate without a bat, as reported in the April 4, 1979 edition of the Paterson Morning Call. The student had struck out seventeen times in a row and the bases were loaded. Edgar told the reporter he figured the kid would be better off without a bat. The pitcher walked the kid in four pitches, which scored the winning run. Right after that, the rule was changed.

The Call also reported a time when one of Cartotto's players was out by a mile as he tried to steal second base. Cartotto ran out to the pitcher's mound and turned to the fans.

"This guy stole every tape deck and hubcap in Paterson last night," he announced, "but today he can't steal second base." Oops!

Edgar denied the story, but an opposing coach claimed it was true.

Other officials who traveled to games across the country with him told us he couldn't sleep unless he kept on the lights and TV in his hotel room—a strange habit. He was a larger-than-life colorful character. We were happy to have known and interacted with Edgar.

Umpiring wasn't his lone extracurricular activity, though. His blood cousin Lou Costello, a fellow Patersonian and half of the famed comedy duo, Abbott and Costello, landed Edgar an occasional gig. During summers in Los Angeles Edgar drove his famous cousin, one of the biggest movie stars of the 1940s, to the most famous Hollywood hot spots. Sometimes Costello brought members of the Rat Pack along for the ride.

"They would call me to drive them around sometimes," Edgar remembered of his association with Frank Sinatra, Dean Martin, Sammy Davis Jr. "It was a real eye-opener, especially for someone my age."[11]

We had many discussions about sports news, rules, and regulations as Edgar ate in the diner. He once told us the best compliment a referee or umpire can get when they work a game is to "have people not realize you're there."

Mike Portella, another character who loved the banter at the Belmont, lived in Haledon for sixty years. On January 6, 1941, he enlisted in the United States Marine Corps and served honorably for six years, fighting in the Solomon Islands and Guadalcanal. When he returned he became a drill instructor at Parris Island, South Carolina. Mike, the resident fuel oil dealer in town, was owner and operator of M. Portella Heating Oil.

Once he gave me a real lesson in oil heating. When I was young I mentioned to him one day that my parents and other friends had said oil heat was dirty and dusty.

"Young man, that is not true," he said. "The dust and dirt come from the type of heating system — either radiators or forced hot air or hot water baseboard. Think about it!"

As I reflected, it made sense that oil burned in the furnace and exhaust left the house via the chimney — another lesson learned from our knowledgeable elder customers.

Mike was a good friend of my dad. They often went to the racetrack together in Monticello, New York.

Pinball Wizards

Bob: To generate more revenue, our father installed a coin-operated pinball machine — an arcade game with a play field in a glass-covered cabinet.

A player pulled a spring plunger in front of the machine, propelling a shiny metal ball, which scored points as it rolled down a slanted surface. A drain, where the ball disappeared at the end of play, was at the bottom. Along the way, though, were paddles called flippers. The player operated the flippers using buttons on each side of the machine. The idea was to keep the play going and score as many points as possible. For a nickel a pinball machine queued up three balls.

When the player scored, the machine generated bright lights and gong sounds. After the last ball dropped in the drain, the game was over — unless you scored enough points to win a replay.

Customers sometimes played pinball for hours. They had a habit of shaking the machine to control the path of the balls. If they shook too hard, though, the "tilt" light came on, the game ended, and a loud shout resounded through the diner, "Oh *%$#.!"

Another standing cigarette machine also generated revenue. A pack cost 25¢.

The Haledon G&M Vending Company installed and maintained the machines. It also shared the

weekly profits. The usual breakdown was 60 percent to G&M, 40 percent to our father.

To further help make ends meet, my dad allowed a road construction company to rent the parking lot. PT&L (Matt Permatti, Paul Tote, and Nick Langanello) parked three of their tan camouflage military-purchased construction trucks in the back. Matt was our Uncle Jerry Rostello's brother-in-law. All three had served in the Seabees, which helped build more than four hundred Naval bases in World War II theaters. Starting their own construction company was a natural outgrowth of the friendship and expertise they developed during the war. Over time PT&L became one of the largest road construction companies in the state.

Another major event was a carnival that set up on the diner grounds. We're not certain if they paid rent or not, but Bob and I helped set up and break down the children's rides they provided. We didn't make much money, but it was lots of fun and we made enough to buy the cotton candy or enjoy some rides.

Bob: We owned a very large empty field behind the diner. Molly Ann Brook ran through it. On the other side of the brook were several vacant dye houses. I'd heard that Ted Williams, the greatest baseball hitter of all time, had practiced hitting small stones with a broomstick. I got into a similar daily routine at the rear of the diner. I tossed small stones in the air and attempted to hit them with a broomstick. Sometimes I hit stones until our father closed the business for the day. I thought this exercise would help my eye-to-

hand coordination over time. It did help me to become a better hitter. Sometimes I swung the broomstick and hit the stone over the brook and onto the roof of a vacant dye house. That, of course, was a home run, which got me very excited. Occasionally, I hit one toward the dye house that fell short of the roof and crashed into one of the windows. When the glass broke, the game was over. It was time to run into the kitchen with the broomstick and hide.

Another vivid memory involves the mice in the basement. Of course, the food on the premises attracted them. My father bought a large cage-style trap that mice could enter to fetch the bait but not escape. When the trap cumulated more than a half dozen mice, we marched to Molly Ann Brook and submerged it in the water, drowning them all. As young as I was and not knowing better, I felt sorry for the little creatures.

At times the employees and customers took turns shooting the larger rats that sometimes roamed the garbage piles some distance behind the diner. They used .22-caliber rifles for this target practice. So my father had two effective methods of dealing with vermin.

One day in the front parking lot, Charles "Junior" Melone, our cousin who worked for our family, swung a long lead pipe in a circle. Somehow I walked into it. I never knew what hit me. My lip was bleeding profusely. My father grabbed a white towel and held it over my face. Instantly, it turned red. He carried me up the street to the barbershop, which had a telephone, and called the Haledon police, who arrived very quickly. They drove me to the emergency room at Paterson General Hospital. By that time the towel was completely bright red.

The doctor sutured me with three stitches from my nose to the bottom of my top lip. Today a cosmetic surgeon would place at least a dozen sutures so as not to leave a scar. My mother was concerned the scar would be very visible when I got older and when I grew a beard. The doctor did such a great job, though, that I have never had anyone ask me about it.

Bob: Everyone at the diner had plenty of quirks. Our dad had an odd habit whenever he brought a sandwich to a customer. Say he had a hamburger on a paper dish. He put his greasy thumb on top of the bun, leaving a print.

"Dad, you can't do that," we said.

"Why?" he replied. "It's just going to fall off the plate otherwise."

One customer with a name recognition problem came in one day.

"Where's Vince?" he asked.

"We don't have a Vince here," Nick answered.

"Yes, your father." Finally, we understood.

"No, they call him 'Finns,' short for Finamore," I said.

When a customer asked for toast and a cup of tea, Finns would say, "What the hell do you think this is? A hospital"?

One of his famous sayings was, "The mills of the Gods grind slowly, but exceedingly fine." For some reason, he also hated making a grilled cheese sandwich for a customer.

One of our short order cooks smoked a cigarette as he worked at the grill. Occasionally, his hacking cough acted up as he prepared the food. One of our breakfast regulars would always order an egg sandwich on white bread. One morning he sat on a stool by the grill and ordered directly with the cook.

"Joe, I want an egg sandwich on white, with only two coughs, please!" Could there be any better example of our customers' loyalty?

Another time Joe handed a customer the spatula and told him to cook the time-consuming dish that he had ordered. While the customer prepared his own food, Joe watched from a stool on the other side of the counter.

You can't make this stuff up!

Chapter 7
Dad Goes to War

J apan, an island nation, got into World War II because it didn't have the natural resources to satisfy its objectives of expansion and rapid growth. They looked to grow by expanding to other lands. On December 7, 1941 they attacked American forces at Pearl Harbor, Hawaii. The next day President Roosevelt famously declared, "Yesterday, December 7, 1941 — a date which will live in infamy — the United States of America was suddenly and deliberately attacked by naval and air forces the Empire of Japan."

The war was focused against three primary evil leaders — Hitler in Germany, Mussolini in Italy, and Hirohito in Japan. People had silhouettes of these three hanging in effigy as a reminder of this "Axis of Evil."

Near the war's end in 1945, the US government envisioned the need to directly confront Japan on its soil. It became so desperate to draft more soldiers that it turned to married men. With that, our father, then thirty-one years old, was sent to Camp Rucker, Alabama for basic training.

He'd been classified as 4F (physically unfit for duty) because of his flat feet, but he was still drafted into the Army.

Finamore family photo

Dad in his Army uniform.

Bob: My mother and I traveled on a train with a steam engine locomotive to Dothan, Alabama to visit my father in boot camp. What surely was a long, exhausting trip for her was fun for a five-year-old. The conductor passed through the passenger cars with sandwiches and cartons of milk or juice. This

was my favorite time during the trip! After finishing each drink, I saved the carton and placed it on the windowsill. By trip's end the sill was filled.

Nick stayed home with my Grandmother Angelina in Astoria, Queens. While there, he contracted chicken pox.

In the South we experienced segregation for the first time. Even the bathrooms were separated. Outside some were signs that read, "Colored Only." No Negroes were allowed in white-owned restaurants in the South, either. When we boarded a bus in Dothan, I ran to the back, as many children do. The driver stopped the bus.

"Your son can't sit there," he told my mother. "Rear seats are for Negroes only."

We had never experienced anything like that in the North.

At the war's end our father was shipped to California, a staging area for the expected invasion of Japan. President Truman decided to end the war, though, by dropping atomic bombs on Hiroshima and Nagasaki. His rationale was that the move would save one million lives on both sides.

Many in our family were drafted into the war, including our Uncle Frank and Jerry Rostello, a cousin of our mother. Jerry, who received a Purple Heart for his wound in the Battle of Guadalcanal, was mentioned in a post-war book about the famous battle. American losses were heavy — 1,592 killed and 4,000 injured out of 60,000 deployed soldiers. The Japanese lost 14,800 soldiers to fighting and another 9,000 to tropical diseases, out of 31,400 soldiers deployed.

Former TV newscaster Tom Brokaw later wrote *The Greatest Generation*, which describes those who lived through the hardships of the Great Depression and then either fought in World War II or worked in the industries that helped win the war. They emerged from all that poverty and sacrifice with invaluable traits they taught us. The nation was not divided in that era at all. All Americans, Democrats and Republicans, pulled closely together to defeat the enemy threats. This generation was "can do" and viewed setbacks as a road to victory. Despite their blood, sweat and tears, the Greatest Generation was humble about what they had done. After the war the cost of living improved.

We were considered the Silent, or Traditionalist, Generation (born 1945 and before). Following us were the Baby Boomers (1946 to 1964), then Generation X (1965 to 1976), and now Millennials or Generation Y (1977 to 1995). Anyone born after 1996 belongs to Generation Z, known as Centennials.

World War II Rationing

There were great shortages of food and other essential commodities during the war. I remember the government rationing sugar, meat, cooking oil, cereals, cheese, eggs, and canned goods. We were given ration books of removable stamps and coupons with expiration dates. At the store we presented them when we purchased certain items to prove we weren't getting more than our fair share. Each person was allowed a certain number of weekly points.

"Red Stamp" rationing covered all meats, butter, fat, and oils, and with some exceptions, cheese. "Blue Stamp" rationing covered canned goods, bottled liquids, frozen fruits and vegetables, dry beans, and processed foods such as soups, baby food, and ketchup. We were asked to conserve everything, so rationing meant sacrifices for all. Few complained, though, because the supplies were going to the Armed Forces and the war effort.

People shared what they had to make things easier for all and to support our troops. The government also asked us to grow our own vegetables. By 1944 the public grew 20 million so-called "victory gardens," which produced some eight million tons of food — more than 40 percent of all the fresh fruits and vegetables Americans ate.[12]

Air Raid Drills

Air raid drills, also known as "blackout" drills, were another fact of life. When alarm sirens went off at night, we shut off all the house lights. To prevent the escape of any light that could aid enemy aircraft, we also pulled down blinds or covered windows with heavy curtains. Air raid wardens cruised down the streets to make certain there were absolutely no lights.

Even streetlights were turned off. We listened to the radio but keep the lighted dial covered.

The idea was that the enemy couldn't target what they couldn't see. We appreciated being asked to take responsibility for protecting ourselves. I think that probably was part of the objective — to mobilize everyone so they felt part of the war effort.

Bob: When the Soviet Union exploded its first atomic bomb in 1949, the American people were understandably nervous. We remembered the destruction caused by the bombs dropped on Hiroshima and Nagasaki. The government created the Civil Defense Administration to educate and reassure the country that there were ways to survive an atomic attack by the Soviet Union. One, called the "Duck and Cover," involved conducting air raid drills in schools. Our teachers yelled, "Drop" and we knelt under our desks with our hands clutched behind our heads. The Civil Defense Administration developed an educational film to instruct all teachers and students.

But we had other personal challenges to face during the war while Dad was away.

The Flood

After our father was drafted into the US Army, my mother kept the diner going so we could continue to make a living. Some family members helped her out.

In 1945, however, a major cataclysmic event struck in my mother's life again. After torrential rains covered large areas of New Jersey and New York, the Bridge's Pond Dam north of Haledon burst, creating a flash flood and overflowing nearby Molly Ann Brook. The brook's source is in High Mountain from which the water winds along Pompton Road and then flows south beside Haledon Avenue. It then crosses Belmont Avenue and continues down to Paterson, where it finds the mouth of the Passaic River just before Paterson's Great Falls.

Used with permission from Haledon 100 Years of History: The Haledon Centennial Book Committee

Haledon flood of 1945. The Belmont Diner is just visible in the distance at the left edge of the photo.

During the flood skeins of silk from Seyer's Silk Finishing and Dyeing Company floated down

Belmont Avenue with the brook's water flow. They caused the Belmont Avenue Bridge to collapse. The raging water reached a level so high it reached the top of our counter in the diner. As a six-year-old kid I remembered I had Crayola brand coloring crayons in the diner. When we entered after the water had subsided, I was upset because the colors had all melded together.

It was a disaster. Our mother dealt with it for six months while our father was in the Army. Some distant cousins pitched in to clean up the mess as well as a number of townspeople, including store owners and neighbors.

Chapter 8
The Babe Comes to Town

George Herman "Babe" Ruth Jr. was on hand to dedicate the Roe Street Field on August 3, 1946. In one corner of the open flat field, shaped like a rectangle, there was a Little League field. In the opposite corner was a regulation baseball diamond. The corner to the left of the baseball diamond contained a flagpole and dedication monument. An individual's home was situated in the corner to the left of the Little League field.

Yankee legend Babe Ruth was on hand for the original dedication of Roe Street Field on August 3, 1946. Pictured with the Bambino is Haledon resident "Babe" Hanner.

Used with permission from Haledon 100 Years of History: The Haledon Centennial Book Committee

Babe Ruth (left) at the Roe Street Field dedication (1946).

Since our home at 429 Roe Street was just a block away, my brother and I walked to the field. We and our father were Yankee fans who admired Joe DiMaggio, Yogi Berra, and Phil Rizzuto, but we weren't aware of Ruth's history with the New York Yankees.

Babe Ruth's career spanned twenty-two seasons from 1914 to 1935. He started as a left-handed pitcher for the Boston Red Sox at $3,500 a season. He pitched twenty-nine scoreless World Series innings. Ruth was traded to the New York Yankees in 1920. For the next eighty-six years, the Red Sox won no championships, giving rise to rumors of a jinx called "Curse of the Bambino."

But the Babe rose to his greatest fame as a slugger for the Yankees. He held the record for most home runs in a single season, earning his nicknames, "The Sultan of Swat" and "The Bambino." He hit sixty homers during the 1927 season, a record that lasted thirty-four years until another New York Yankee, Roger Maris, broke it by hitting sixty-one homers during the 1961 season.

His fame and talent reached such a high level in 1930 and 1931 that he was paid $80,000 a year, $5,000 more than the president of the United States at the time.

In the summer of 1946, when he came to Haledon, Ruth suffered with severe pain over his left eye—a condition diagnosed that November as cancer.[13] When he arrived in our hometown, though, no one could tell he was in pain. He arrived in a black chauffeur-driven limo and shed a long black coat because it was a warm summer day. His wife and one of his daughters accompanied him. He was dressed in a white shirt with long sleeves that he folded up. We remember him as big and earthy with a deep voice.

They placed a microphone on the pitcher's mound from which Ruth talked about how, at age seven, he entered the St. Mary's Industrial School for Boys in Baltimore and stayed for twelve years. There he was mentored by Xaverian Brother Matthias, who taught him to pitch, catch, and hit. He praised Brother Matthias, whose running and hitting styles closely resembled his.

Hour after hour, he explained, Brother Mathias made him stand in the corner of the field and catch bunted balls to learn hand-eye coordination. He said Brother Matthias helped him turn his life around, walk away from a troublemaking youth, and choose a career in baseball—another example of how a close mentoring relationship can influence another individual's life. The August 5, 1946 edition of the *Paterson Morning Call* quoted Ruth as saying, "...that juvenile delinquency could be licked by giving the children proper sports facilities for clean, wholesome play."

That day Ruth covered highlights of his career with both the Red Sox and Yankees, too. He also said he'd like to be invited back the following year to see the field with bleachers and other improvements.

After he spoke, he set up a batter and catcher on the left side of the backstop and on the right side another batter and catcher at their respective simulated home plates. He then took up a position on the pitcher's mound with two baseballs in his left hand.

"This is the how I pitched a double header in one game," he said.

He wound up and threw the two balls at the same time to each battery. The catchers within the strike zone caught both baseballs. He did it twice. The crowd was amazed. Since that demonstration we have never seen anyone achieve this feat.

I met his granddaughter, Linda Ruth Tosetti, at a memorabilia expo in November 2019 and I told her the story. She had never heard of him doing that.

After his demonstration Ruth sat on the dais/ grandstand at the engraved stone monument and signed autographs for the estimated one thousand attendees. I was a seven-year-old kid standing at the foot of the grandstand. Ed Romanelli, a town police officer, asked me if I wanted an autograph. I nodded.

He then picked me up and placed me on the grandstand. Babe Ruth signed his autograph in pencil on a piece of paper. I still have it today. It hasn't faded for seventy-three years. As seen in the photo on the next page, I've mounted it in a shadow box behind museum glass for preservation.

Finamore family photo

Babe Ruth display, including autograph.

Joe DiMaggio Autograph

I missed the start of Little League Baseball when it was instituted in America, but Bob played in the Haledon Recreation League. Little League had tryouts for major and minor league teams. Not everyone made the team of their choice. Those who didn't had to learn to live with the disappointment.

Bob: I was in the last inning of a playoff game with the other team's tying run on third base. Their batter was up with two outs. I was the catcher. With two strikes on the batter, the pitcher wound up and threw the ball. The batter swung. I heard the ball tip the bat. However, the umpire called the batter out. The opposing coach complained.

The umpire asked me if the batter had tipped the ball.

"Yes, he did," I said.

On the next pitch the batter swung and missed, which ended the game with a 6–5 win for my team.

My coach picked up on what I'd done. Since we were playing in the Paterson Old Timers Baseball League, he told the league about this example of outstanding sportsmanship. League officials presented me with a baseball signed by Joe DiMaggio at a ceremony before a game at the Roe Street Field. My father, mother and brother were there.

Unfortunately, unlike the Babe Ruth autograph, the DiMaggio signature was in ballpoint pen and has faded so much over time, it's not recognizable.

YMCA Home Vacation Camp

As we got older, both parents continued to work in the diner to reduce employee expenses. When we were out of school in summertime, they sent us to the

Finamore family photo

Bob receives a ball autographed by Yankee great Joe DiMaggio.
Left to right: Nick, Mom, Bob, Dad.

YMCA in Paterson and a camp called the Home Vacation Camp.

They dropped us off in the morning and picked us up in the afternoon so it was a whole day split up into four major activities — pool swimming, arts and crafts, gym, lunch, and sometimes an uphill hike to Garret Mountain. which was five miles away.

When our father first took us, we asked him if we needed to bring our bathing suits.

"No, you don't need them," he said. In those days the men at the Y swam with no suits and only needed to shower before entering the pool. We were shocked. Many of the men would jump up and down on the swimming board before diving in. You might envision what a sight that was!

During our time in the pool, we both learned to swim and passed water tests on specific levels of achievement.

We made many friends at the Y. We all sang our favorite camper songs. Here is one:

*We are the Home Vacation Camp, the camp we love
so well.*

Whenever we go out, the happy people shout,

Hey! Here comes the Home Vacation Camp.

DaDaDaDaDaDaDaaaa

And another:

I'm a hayseed, my hair is seaweed

*And my ears are made of leather and they flap in
windy weather*

*I'm made of Hemlock, tough as a pine nut. I'm a Y
camper, don't you see?*

When we arrived in the morning, we assembled and sang other songs, such as "Faith of Our Fathers." We didn't know the melody or words but we sang as loud as we could. We had fun!

Bob and I and our close buddy, Bobby Thompson, who was a great swimmer, decided to pull a stunt on Smiley Schultz, another camper. We convinced Smiley that my nickname was "The Gouge" and that if I didn't like someone, I gouged their eye out with one finger.

One day we had a little closed box with cotton in it. On it was a marble—an eyeball--with red paint to simulate blood. We attached pieces of strings to simulate nerves and muscle tissue, too. It was our way of convincing Smiley that "The Gouge" did exist.

The next day we brought the box to camp and called over Smiley.

"'The Gouge' just took another eye out," I said. When we opened the box, he freaked out. Smiley didn't want to go near me for the rest of the year, but he was a wonderful fellow camper and a close friend.

Smiley couldn't swim as well as Bobby Thompson. Nor could we, although we became more proficient over time. We started at the shallow end of the pool and learned to kick with our feet as we held onto the side. We learned the "Australian Crawl" stroke, too. Once we could swim proficiently across the pool, we were tested at swimming the length. Since it was an Olympic-size pool, that was about eighty-two feet.

We then graduated to the deep end of the pool, where more advanced swimming and diving techniques challenged us.

Bob: At the end of camp the counselors nominated the best camper of the year, taking into account the gym, swimming, and overall good conduct. The winner was announced at the end-of-year parents' celebration and award ceremony. I was a finalist.

The day before decision time, however, I exited the swimming pool, rolled my towel into a "rat's tail," flicked it at another camper, and hit him on the behind. Unfortunately, one of the counselors saw it.

That was it! I was disqualified and out of the running for the camper of the year.

I was honored, though, with an individual tribe award at the parents' night ceremony, ending the eight-week YMCA summer camp.

At parents' night we put on skits in the gymnasium that we thought were funny. In one skit a camper walked across the floor to another camper on the other side.

"Do you have it yet?" the first camper asked. The other camper had a bag full of objects. He pulled all of them out of the bag.

"No, I don't have it!" he said, before departing.

The routine repeated many more times while the first camper got more and more visibly distressed. He crawled across the floor in discomfort and asked once again.

"Do you have it now?"

At that moment the second camper again went through his bag and finally pulled out a roll of toilet paper. At that point the first camper jumped off the gym floor, screamed joyously, grabbed the roll, and ran toward the gym exit door leading to the bathroom.

In another skit we put up a sheet with a light projected behind it. The audience saw the silhouette of a camper lying on a table. Next other campers, pretending to be doctors, started an operation during which they pulled out chains, balls, an enema bag, various tools, and other objects. The camper on the table, playing the patient, was encouraged to scream loudly. If he didn't, some of the "doctors" pinched him for "encouragement." Laugh!

In yet another skit several campers argued in the middle of the gymnasium floor. As the banter continued, one broke away and ran out of the gym with the others in hot pursuit. The camper who ran off suddenly appeared on the elevated track some 25 or 30 feet above the gymnasium floor. While he was chased, he tripped and fell behind a dark curtain draped over the track railing. The pursuing campers caught up and also disappeared behind the curtain.

Sounds of a scuffle ensued. Soon a body was thrown over the railing onto the gym floor. The audience screeched, screamed, gasped, laughed, and we even heard some exclaim, "Oh my God!" No harm, no foul. There was a dummy behind the curtain dressed exactly like the camper.

Getaway at Silver Lake

We enrolled for a weekend YMCA outing in Silver Lake in North Jersey. We brought food, including one of our dad's diner staples, Trenton Taylor Pork Roll. (In New Jersey — especially North Jersey — we call it Taylor Ham.)

On the first day of camp, we cooked the Taylor Ham in a frying pan over an open firepit. As soon as we started, a heavy rainstorm came through, filling the frying pan with water and dousing the fire. We were very disappointed and hungry since we had no alternate food source. We didn't think things could get any worse — until that night.

On the way to our cabins to turn in, our counselors called all the campers together for a meeting. They said one of the campers had wet one of the counselor's beds. They wanted to know who did it. They kept us outside most of the night and into the wee hours, but no one fessed up. We were even told scary ghost stories in an attempt to get someone to confess.

To compound these unfortunate experiences, the weather continued to be terrible for the entire weekend and the lake, full of weeds, was not conducive to swimming. Not a fun weekend at Silver Lake! All in all, it was a terrible experience for us boys. When we got home and explained what happened, our mother concluded we'd just been homesick.

Chapter 9
Across the River

We stayed close to Grandpa and Grandma Carnevale after they moved to Astoria, Queens, New York. Grandpa was always dressed in a suit with a white shirt, tie, and vest. He wore a railroad-style pocket watch on a gold chain that he tucked into pockets on either side of his vest. It extended across his middle section through a vest buttonhole. Though his job as a

Finamore family photo
Grandpa Carnevale (1919).

weaver must have been messy, he dressed formally and with great elegant fashion when he wasn't at work. He was short. I don't recall him wearing glasses on any occasion.

Our grandparents rented in a row house in a lineup of similar houses, each with three-step stoops. Theirs, made of amber and blond bricks, sat on a street corner. They had to walk up to their second-floor apartment. Grandma was very cautious in this new environment, so they locked the entrance door at the bottom. To let someone in, they had to walk down the long flight of stairs to open the front door.

Their small railroad apartment had a kitchen, dining room, and two bedrooms with one bathroom — and a unique bathroom at that. The toilet water tank was ceiling height. To flush we pulled on a chain hanging from the tank.

We four, along with Grandma and Grandpa, usually ate with our Uncle Tom and Aunt Rita, cousins Tommy and Linda, and Uncle Frank and Uncle Al. That made twelve people sitting around a small table in a small dining room — the Italian way! It was so tight that cousin Tommy remarked one day that we were there to "kiss the wallpaper." We all laughed.

Many Sundays, our family traveled by car from Haledon to spend the day with the family. We drove across the Washington and Triborough bridges to enter Queens. In the earlier days my parents drove to a New Jersey port and took the automobile ferry across the Hudson River to Queens.

Our grandmother was a good cook and we always enjoyed a traditional-style Italian meal that went on for hours. It started with antipasto and moved to soup, then pasta served with meatballs and sausage, then the entrée of meat or fish. Our grandfather sat at the head of the table. The salad, which always came last, usually was dressed with red vinegar and olive oil.

We always had red wine. Our grandfather served us small portions at an early age. Most Italians drank wine because the drinking water in Italy was so poor. Also, the great soil and climate, especially in Tuscany, was conducive to growing quality vineyard grapes.

Finamore family photo

Family dinner at Grandpa and Grandma Carnevale's house.
Left to right: Dad, Nick, Bob, Uncle Frank, Grandpa Alphonso, Grandma
Angelina, Aunt Rita Carnevale (Uncle Tom's wife), Mom, baby cousin Tommy
Carnevale (Rita's son). 1944.

The grown-ups discussed politics and religion, the news topics of the day, and life in general. We listened intently. Every so often, they asked us about school or sports activities. I'm convinced we assimilated teachings on morality and core family values at those meals.

Our grandmother always got dessert and baked goods from Walken's Bakery—a variety of cannolis, Napoleons, sfogliatella and other low-calorie, low-fat treats. Ha! But they were all delicious.

We always had so much food that we left with bags of leftovers to take home. One day all the bags were on the table. We grabbed a couple. When we arrived home we discovered we'd taken their garbage.

Every time we started to leave the apartment, our grandfather attempted to give us one dollar each. Of course we feinted and said, "No, thank you." He always insisted, though, as we knew he would. We caved and took it. Every time!

All their lives my grandparents never owned a car or drove or obtained a driver's license. The elevated subway, called the El, was a block from their house. Besides, in Astoria all the stores were very close. Grandma and Grandpa walked to all of them. They only took the subway when they needed to get to a distant location.

Contadina Thermostat

During one winter meal we noticed a small Contadina tomato paste can tied to the thermostat that controlled the steam heat for the apartment.

"What's that all about?" I asked Grandpa.

He said the stingy landlord wouldn't heat the apartment to the set level in the winter. So Grandpa put ice in the can and tied it to the thermostat. That way they got plenty of heat. It worked!

In Astoria our grandparents could walk or ride the subway to wherever they needed to go. The grocery store was one block away and Walken's Bakery, owned by the parents of actor Christopher Walken, was also a short walk away. I got to stay with Grandpa and Grandma Carnevale for two summers because our parents worked together in the diner business. Before the war few married women were in the workforce though that changed dramatically afterwards.

But our grandparents lived in the ways they brought here from Italy. Grandpa was the breadwinner, the one who worked outside the home and economically supported the family. Grandma Carnevale was the homemaker and had complete responsibility for running the house, including cleaning, washing and drying clothes, ironing, shopping, and cooking.

I was a boy from the suburbs. Living in the city was very different, but I became very fond of city life.

Grandpa and Grandma took me to the Astoria pool. My favorite memory with them was enjoying an ice cream bar after dinner. A vendor named the Bungalow Bar drove down the street, pulled to the curb, and sold ice cream bars off the truck. His vehicle was built to look like a bungalow house with a shingled roof, windows, and a door.

Even though Grandma Carnevale spent part of her childhood in a convent, she didn't discern a calling to become a nun. She became very religious and could recite the Catholic Mass in Latin from start to finish. In the '60s she was disappointed when they changed to local languages. Another experience from her convent years traumatized her, though. One day lightning struck the convent, starting a fire. All her life, Grandma was unnerved whenever a thunderstorm passed through.

A short woman who wore glasses, she lived her role as a wife and mother with dignity and joy. She was very outgoing and easily made friends with the neighbors and storekeepers she dealt with daily.

She told us she slept only two to three hours a night. Was that the reason she lived to 102? Or was it because of Haledon's "Fountain of Youth"?

Sleepless in Astoria

Much as I liked Astoria, it took some time to get accustomed to the noise when sleeping. Every ten minutes a subway rumbled past on the El. There was no air conditioning, either—only screens in the windows during summer days.

Grandpa and Grandma Carnevale also lived very close to LaGuardia Airport. That was the era of prop planes, which sounded like they were coming through the bedroom. The street noise was constant, too, including milk deliveries in the early morning hours. Eventually, I got accustomed to it.

Their street was never dull. One day a body was discovered in the alleyway next to my grandparents' home. Police determined that it was a mob hit. Another time a manhole exploded in the middle of the night. I was at my grandparents' place in 1945 when a B-25 bomber hit the Empire State Building, then the tallest building in the world, and exploded, killing three people in the plane and eleven working in the building. The bomber was flying from Massachusetts to LaGuardia Airport on a foggy day. When the plane arrived in New York visibility was near zero. The crash was horrifying.

In the city there was always some traumatic event versus the more peaceful life we enjoyed in the suburbs. I remember vividly, though, when my grandparents came to stay with us in Haledon. After the first night my grandmother told us she couldn't sleep in New Jersey. The crickets kept her up!

Yet each side of the river had its wonders. A favorite New York memory was the day my grandfather took me to Coney Island on the subway. I'll never forget it. After we had pizza for lunch, he placed me on a pony ride. Horses fascinated me so that was quite a thrill.

We didn't try the Coney Island Parachute Jump, a popular amusement ride originally designed to train soldiers. The ride featured a steel 250-foot, open-frame tower with twelve cantilever steel arms radiating from the top. Each arm supported a parachute held open by metal rings and attached to a lift rope and a set of cables. Riders were strapped into a canvas seat, two at a time, lifted to the top, and then dropped to slowly descend by parachute. Shock absorbers at the bottom helped everyone land smoothly. It was a sight to watch the passengers' reactions when they were dropped.

I remember it all—the Nathan's hot dog stand, the large amusement area—but mostly spending time with my grandfather, Alphonse, one-on-one.

To keep us occupied Uncle Frank took us on a short drive to LaGuardia Airport where we got close enough to the planes to observe the passengers board or disembark on portable steps—a gangway of stairs. In those days we could view major airlines like TWA and American Airlines and others boarding passengers, cranking two- or four-propeller engines, and taxiing out to the runway. I was mesmerized. I loved flying.

The family found out Grandma Angelina was related to Lou Costello's Aunt May. When the aunt heard I had rheumatic fever at five years old, she told her nephew. Lou Costello sent me an autographed photo of himself that read, "To Nicholas Finamore, From Your Pal, Lou Costello." I still have that photo today.

Lou was fond of the city where he was raised and mentioned Paterson in all his performances. He was most famous for his "Who's On First" routine, a baseball comedy act he performed with his partner, Bud Abbott.

Our grandparents only occasionally spoke their native Italian language in front of us. They loved this country and were dedicated to being American and speaking English. If they wanted to keep a secret from us, though, they spoke Italian. Both of our parents were conversant in Italian, too.

Finamore family photo
Autographed photo of comic great and distant cousin Lou Costello.

Chapter 10
Barbour Street

In 1948 our parents bought a house on Barbour Street, across town, from Charlie Calabrese, a builder who was constructing another house nearby for himself and his wife. Our father was well liked and well known so Calabrese offered our parents the house for fifty dollars per month on a handshake. There was no formal paperwork.

Each month Bob walked to the builder's house one block away and handed him fifty dollars in cash. There was no receipt—just trust. For ten years our parents paid faithfully until they owned the place.

In 1949 my parents bought a new black Oldsmobile Dynamic 88 with lots of chrome. At the time this lightweight two-door sedan was one of the fastest cars in America. It had a 135 hp V8 engine. Named "Futuramic" and "Rocket 88," it accelerated from 0 to 60 mph in thirteen seconds with a top speed of 97

Finamore family photo

Our house on Barbour Street.

mph—a turtle's pace compared to today's perfor-
mance. I'm certain our parents bought the Dynamic 88
Olds because it was popular, not because it was known
as a muscle car.

It was one of the first cars to have an automatic
transmission, called Hydromatic—a major departure
from the manual gear shifts up to then. It had vents
under the headlights, a rocket hood ornament, a trunk
lid emblem, dashboard clock, and spring suspension.
The driver's side and passenger seats tilted forward,
allowing passengers to get into the rear seats. There
were no directional signals so one had to place their
arm out the window and point in the direction they
were turning.

Our garage, which had a substantial-sized porch
over it, faced Barbour Street. The distance from the

garage door to the street was approximately twenty feet. When our Oldsmobile was parked in the driveway, part of it blocked the sidewalk.

We entered our house two ways — through the rear door or the garage. To get to the rear, we went on the right side of the house via a walkway. A few steps led up to the kitchen and double that amount led down to the basement.

The garage entrance was unfinished. It contained the washer and dryer. A small utility room to the rear and left contained the oil burner. The washing machine was a Bendix front loader bolted to a concrete pad on the floor because of the vibration that occurred during the spin cycle. Next to it was a slop sink.

There was also a finished portion to the left with a small bar. Later we added an upright piano. We often used this room, with knotty pine paneling, for band practice. We also used it for parties, including a memorable New Year's Eve gathering with friends and family. Bob and I acted as pseudo bartenders although we were minors at the time.

Heading upstairs took you to the kitchen where the table, now called retro, sported chrome legs and a red enamel top. The six chairs around the table had similar chrome legs and red vinyl seats. This ensemble was on a linoleum floor.

We had the usual toaster, mixers, cookie jar, and canisters holding flour and sugar and other dry bulk foods. In the summer we used stand-up fans.

The living room in front of the house had an entertainment console with a small sixteen-inch TV with no remote control. Our family purchased a magnifier, a glass enclosure filled with water and mounted in front of the TV. It was supposed to make the picture appear larger. Since it wasn't effective, we didn't use it long.

Finamore family photo

Barbour Street house living room.

Bob and I were introduced to TV a couple of years earlier when we watched mostly cowboy shows on relatives' sets. Our father also took us to the local furniture store where we could stand on the sidewalk and watch the TV sets in the window displays. That's where we saw Joe Louis fight Jersey Joe Walcott for the heavyweight championship in 1947. In that fight Louis summoned his legendary power and hit Walcott with a right to the jaw that knocked him unconscious.

Watching TV at home was much more convenient even though we had to get up to change the channel manually. At least there were only three major ones —

Channel 2 (CBS), Channel 4 (NBC), and Channel 7 (ABC). Most of the time we left the TV on one channel because we were too lazy to get up. Other times our grandmother and mom would direct us. "Change the channel!" they'd say.

We sat on either the large tufted sofa or two tufted chairs, one made from Scalamandre silk material that Grandpa Carnevale had produced in the factory in Queens. Several standing floor lamps provided lighting.

The entertainment console had a phonograph that played 78 rpm hard vinyl discs. I listened to many of the big bands, such as Glenn Miller, Duke Ellington, and the Dorsey Brothers. It was here my interest in jazz music began. On the radio we listened to Amos 'n' Andy, Bing Crosby, and the serial programs I described earlier.

For entertainment we also played board games, including Monopoly, and a variety of card games, including Gin Rummy, Canasta, Go Fish, Old Maid, and Pinochle.

Our rotary telephone, which was black (the only color available), sat on a telephone table with a drawer that held a rather large telephone directory. When the phone rang we picked it up without knowing who was calling. Amazing! If we wanted to place a long-distance call, we waited until after 7 p.m. when the rates were lower.

The adjacent dining room had a large polished mahogany table with ornate chairs and a dish closet buffet. A chandelier hung over the table. On the walls were a large mirror and a number of smaller paintings. Usually, a wax floral arrangement was set over a small ornamental crocheted doily mat on the table.

Our bedroom was adjacent to the kitchen. We had heavy maple twin beds and a maple chest of drawers with a shelf that pulled down. The shelf, which served as a desk, contained cubbyholes for storage on the inside. My grandchildren inherited this bedroom ensemble, which is still in use as of this writing.

Since we were next to the kitchen, we smelled the great aroma of meatballs and Italian "gravy" on Sunday mornings. Both our parents were very hard workers. When they opened their diner, they worked six days a week. Their only day off was Sunday. So in our preschool years, they enrolled us in Saint Michael's Church School in Paterson. Each day one of them dropped us off at school where we spent most of the day indoors doing schoolwork.

Bob: Our parents asked us one day what we had for lunch. We said we had a slice of Wonder Bread in a bowl, with chocolate milk poured over it. Aghast, they did not believe us. They thought we were making it up because we didn't like the school. But we were telling the truth. For many days that's exactly what they served for lunch. And we truly did not like the school. Maybe our strange meal was a sign of poverty, a way for Saint Michael's to cut costs and make ends meet.

One of the highlights of our days back then was the jelly roll cakes they sold us in the afternoon. Another was the penny candy we could purchase for one cent. **One of the nuns was in charge of holding open a large box containing the candy. We got to choose what we wanted as we exited the school.**

Food Heaven

But nothing compared to the food we ate at home. Basically, we grew up in food heaven. On Sundays our mother had the greatest ritual. She started by placing a large pot on the stove over high heat. She poured extra virgin olive oil on the bottom of the pot and added onions, minced cloves of garlic, salt, and pepper. The strong, mouthwatering aroma of those ingredients melding together wafted into the nearby bedroom.

After the ingredients were sufficiently sautéed, she added two large cans of Progresso crushed tomatoes with a can of tomato paste. We heard a grand sizzle pop as she poured the tomatoes into the hot oil. (See "Family Recipes" section.)

She made the meatballs with three different kinds of meats for flavor—sausage, pork, and beef. She seasoned the meat with salt, pepper, oregano, and parsley. Then she added eggs and bread soaked in milk, along with breadcrumbs. She kneaded the mixture with her hands, putting in some additional breadcrumbs until firm. The meatballs then were rolled to around two inches in size before she coated them with breadcrumbs and browned them in a skillet. She didn't cook them fully because she submerged them in the gravy where they cooked for two to two-

and-a-half hours. Our mother added some dried basil leaves (*vasanigol*) to the concoction.

She also sautéed hot and sweet sausage, along with *braciole* (pronounced *bra ' zhul*), in the frying pan. She didn't overly cook them, either, because they were also added to the gravy. (See "Family Recipes" section.)

Preparing the *braciole*, made from rolled-up beef or flank steak, took time in itself. The meat was pounded flat to tenderize it and layered with minced garlic, parsley, breadcrumbs, salt, and pepper. The meat was then rolled into a cylinder. Its sides were tucked in to hold the filling in place and secured with string or toothpicks. The greatest joy was dunking crusty bread into the gravy and thanking the Lord for this great Italian food!

Our mother's other signature dish was eggplant parmesan. Both our grandmother Angelina and Grandma Terri Finamore made a similar casserole influenced by cooking in Caserta. Our mother's version was a combination of layers—some of bread stuffing and some of eggplant, peeled and cut lengthwise. The key step was cutting the eggplant into half-inch slices and then placing it on a towel in a colander with a heavy weight. (See "Family Recipes" section.)

Though both our parents worked in the diner, they had dinner with us as often as they could.

Bocce

Whenever we walked down Barbour Street, we stopped and watched the older Italian men play bocce ball on the Piedmont Social Club's outside court. We not only observed how the game was played but learned some Italian by listening to their profanity-laced banter. After they rolled a ball they ran down the length of the court and yelled, "Kiss the *balline* (the small white ball)." In the meantime, they put some body English on the ball with a roll of their torso, pelvis, and hips. We also learned the look and aroma of the Italian Stogie cigar. Watching their games inspired me later in life to build my own bocce court at my summer residence on Cape Cod.

Devil's Den

"Devil's Den" was a mountainous three-acre woodland on an extremely steep embankment behind our house. It stretched from Central Avenue, high above, down to Barbour Street. We liked walking through this small forest though the paths were overgrown with grasses, shrubs, and underbrush. There was still plenty of sunlight and good space among the trees. We never saw any large animals such as deer or bear but there were plenty of squirrels, chipmunks, and snakes. We called it "The Woods" and never found out why it was known as "Devil's Den." It's a mystery to this day.

We had great times in this forest. On snowy, wintry days we sledded down the man-made paths. Before we went outside we put on a pair of socks and covered them with wax paper or Saran Wrap, providing enough insulation for a whole day of sledding in freezing temperatures. We never had cold feet! The trails were intertwined with thick tree roots, making bumps great for sled jumps and thrilling sleigh rides.

The rest of the year, we built forts constructed from lumber we collected from our playmates' houses. We swung on vines from tree to tree, emulating Tarzan and hollering Johnny Weissmuller's distinctive call right from the movies.

One day we were playing army games because we were so influenced by what we'd seen during World War II. Like all boys of that time, we played soldiers. We went out with a crew of eight to ten guys and hiked up north of Devil's Den into an area with high and dry buffalo grass.

One day we built a campfire in a rock-made pit and cooked baked beans and other food. Since it was very windy, the buffalo grass caught fire.

"Take off your coats and fight the fire!" said Jack Faller, one of our group. He swung his into the flames, trying to beat down the blaze. I attempted the same thing, but when I swatted the fire, it reflected back to me and burnt my eyebrows off.

In no time flames engulfed the entire field. We picked up our gear and ran home. Since our father was the fire chief, we were scared to death. He would not be happy that his children started a brush fire in town.

On our way back, we dropped a bunch of paraphernalia down a hill and ran home. Our friends told us later that it looked like we had dropped off the earth. For whatever reason, when we got inside, we took our clothes off and got into our beds.

When our father got home, he didn't think much of what happened except for our missing eyebrows. It turned out to be a small brush fire, easily put out. Whew! Dodged that bullet.

More Pranks

"Goosey Night" was one of the most fun nights ever. Where did the name come from? Who knows? In many areas across the country the night before Halloween was called "Mischief Night." Whatever it's called, it was a time to pull pranks on neighbors. As an example, we soaped up car and store windows. We also placed dog doo-doo in a bag, doused it with lighter fluid, and placed it on someone's porch by their front door. Then we rang the doorbell and hid, hoping that when the homeowner came out, they'd stomp on the fire. Most of the time the neighbors, familiar with the trick, didn't even try to extinguish the blaze. Disappointing!

Bob: We executed other pranks from the second-floor attic windows of our home. They faced to the side and out directly to the street. We filled balloons with water and waited, one of us stationed at each window. When a car drove up the street, the boy

observing out the side window signaled at a certain point. We exactly timed the throw out the front window so the filled balloon would hit the front windshield of a passing automobile. Drivers got out of their cars but didn't see anyone.

One time when I was the thrower, I launched the balloon at the signal of the lookout. Unfortunately, I miscalculated and the balloon hit the inside frame of the window, showering us pranksters with water. Nice try!

On Halloween night we had even more fun. We dressed in costumes and went into the town parade, marching from Kossuth Street down to Absalom Grundy School, where we passed a line of judges who picked the best costumes. The chosen individuals won a prize. Afterwards, everyone enjoyed cider and doughnuts at the field.

For the remainder of the night, we went trick or treating, just as it is done today.

Another fun activity was sneaking into Camp Veritan's pool to take a dip on oppressive summer nights. We tried to keep quiet, but inevitably made enough noise to alert the neighbors, who called the Haledon Police Department. Upon hearing the siren, we rapidly exited the pool and scattered. Lucky for us we never got caught.

Haledon Fire Department

A volunteer member of the Haledon Fire Department for years, our father became chief in 1946 and 1947. We were very proud when he gave his speech at the Labor Day ceremony, a fundraiser for the firehouse. The day included a parade down Belmont Avenue. We got to ride one of the two fire trucks from the #1 firehouse—either "The Fox" or "The Diamond T." We were allowed to press the siren button as we proceeded down Belmont Avenue.

Finamore family photo

Dad giving his Labor Day speech.

The parade ended at the A&P parking lot on Belmont Avenue. There, next to Molly Ann Brook, was a large tent with picnic and games set up for the whole town. The most special food offering was a very large black kettle over an open fire. The kettle contained gallons of homemade Manhattan clam chowder.

We took dry ice from the ice cream concession and placed portions of it into Molly Ann Brook, where it bubbled and smoked. A fascinating scientific observation!

The other big fundraiser for the firehouse was "Donkey Softball," played on a softball diamond behind Absalom Grundy School. Two teams of firemen played a regular game of softball with all players—except the pitcher, catcher and batter—mounted on specially trained donkeys. When the batter made a hit, he had to mount a live donkey and make his way around the bases on its back. The promoter provided uncooperative donkeys with minds of their own. They frequently stopped short, sometimes throwing their riders off their bare backs. The players in the field needed to dismount to pick up balls and then remount.

Hometown fans delighted in watching their favorite firemen perform with all their hijinks and "trash talk," as we call it today. Of course, the two teams constantly harassed each other. We all had a barrelful of laughs!

Typically, a loud horn that could be heard across our one-square-mile town alerted the Haledon volunteer firemen of an alarm. The horn blasted in code: the first set of blasts represented a number, as did the second set. For instance, one blast meant "1" and three quick blasts in a row meant "3." The firemen knew where Box 13 was in town. Some raced to the firehouse to drive the engines while others went directly to the alarm box.

When Box 13 was sounded, our father jumped out of bed, quickly put on his clothes, and headed directly to the diner. That code was the signal for the alarm box close to his business. Sometimes he waited for the No. 2 firehouse truck, which was near us, to stop by and pick him up on its way.

One day we heard the fire horn blare out "1-3" and saw smoke coming from the Haledon Bank up the street from the diner. I walked up Belmont Avenue from the diner to see what was going on. As I got within twenty-five yards, my eyes burned. When the irritation became very painful, I ran back toward the diner. Once I was at a safe distance from the bank, I stopped and continued to observe.

Haledon Fire Department's Fox fire truck came hurtling down Belmont Avenue at great speed and stopped in front of the bank. Fireman Lou Coral, wearing his fire jacket, jumped off the running board and ran through the bank's front doors. Within seconds he came running back out, covering his tearing eyes. I don't think that gas masks or respirators were part of their firefighting equipment in those days.

We'd always heard a rumor that the Haledon Bank could activate tear gas when a robbery was taking place to neutralize the criminals.

Three or four bank employees hung their heads out the front window and coughed violently. After a time, the tear gas dissipated and things settled down. It turned out to be a false alarm, but we then knew the rumor was true. We heard later that the bank removed the tear gas system and put in another set of deterrents.

Bob: My father told us about a night fire he fought at the Gaiz's farm stables. This was during World War II. Through the firefighters' heroic efforts, most of the livestock was saved though several horses were lost.

He also talked about the day he drove Henry Esselman's milk truck and a bakery truck struck him in the left rear. The milk truck overturned, flooding the streets with milk and littering the intersection with broken bottles. Our father, who was dazed and injured, got first aid. He was ordered to bed and observed. The bakery truck driver was given a summons for reckless driving.

One day our father took me to the scene of a major automobile accident that had occurred the night before.

"Nick," he said, "come with me."

A car with three World War II veterans was speeding down Snake Hill Road, which, as the name implies, was steep and winding. They were making a right turn onto another road when the car skidded and hit a telephone pole on the left. One man was thrown from the car and impaled high up on the pole. (There were no seat belts back then.) I saw some of the remains still present. The sight had the effect our father intended. That scene has been embedded in my memory for all time. I didn't need a safe driving course after that.

For many years our father said that, as a retired fireman, he was "exempt." We never knew what that meant until he passed away in 2000: all his substantial funeral expenses were paid.

Chapter 11
New Friends, New Fun

We both attended Kossuth Street School until we moved. Then we went to Absalom Grundy Elementary School, about a hundred yards down Barbour Street and across the street from our house. I started third grade there while Bob began second.

We learned and sang a great poem about the school. It was really a classic nursery rhyme about Solomon Grundy, a fictional character who lives and dies his entire life in one week, but we substituted "Absalom" for "Solomon":

Absalom Grundy,
Born on a Monday,
Christened on Tuesday,
Married on Wednesday,
Took ill on Thursday,
Grew worse on Friday,
Died on Saturday,

Buried on Sunday,
That was the end,
Of Absalom Grundy.

The school was named for a teacher who taught in Haledon for thirty-eight years from 1893 to 1931. We studied at Absalom Grundy through sixth grade. After we moved to Wayne Township in 1958, they changed the school's name to Haledon Public School. But the name Absalom Grundy is still etched into the concrete facade above the Barbour Street entrance.

We started each day by reciting "The Pledge of Allegiance" to the United States of America. We placed our hand over our heart and recited the words, including "one nation under God." Because of the war effort and our upbringing, we were patriotic. We appreciated capitalism and America as a country — "the land of the free and home of the brave."

Courtesy of American Labor Museum / Botto House National Landmark
Absalom Grundy Elementary School.

In those days when we weren't in the woods behind our house, we were playing, unsupervised, in the Absalom Grundy field, which was the length of three football fields.

School Days

We developed many great friendships over the years and came across many different personalities. One of the most memorable for me was a boy not named here. He was one of the most uncoordinated individuals I've ever met. He had near zero eye-hand coordination. He probably had Asperger's Syndrome or another developmental disorder identified in later years. But he was extremely intelligent. I envied him because he could say the alphabet backwards and had a fantastic math capability. He was also obsessed with collecting things, especially cigarette packs. He found them on the streets, even rare brands like "Wings" that no one had heard of.

Many boys in the school were natural athletes like Gary Kamphouse, a terrific baseball and softball player who was also quarterback on the football team.

I felt sorry for another kid I'll call Rudy Wolfgang, whose family was from Germany. One teacher accused him of hitting some girls and scolded him fiercely in front of the class. His family was extremely courteous, though. His mother baked and shared outstanding German Streusel Cakes. As I reflect now, I think the teacher's *animus* was left over from our hatred of Nazis in World War II.

Our teachers also were unique individuals with much different personalities. We called most of our female teachers "Miss" because we never knew if they were married. Our fourth-grade teacher had an upright piano in her class and she was classically trained to play it. If a student was disruptive in class, she placed them behind the piano, against the wall, and played a loud classical piece. I daresay that in this day and age she would've been arrested.

Finamore family photo

*Fourth grade class. Bob is just to the right of center,
with his right hand holding the top of his book.*

Our fifth-grade teacher told us she had eyes in the back of her head. To demonstrate she faced away from the class, toward the blackboard, and told us to perform some movement or action. She then played back to us what we did. Pure magic!

Finamore family photo

Fifth grade class. Nick is on the left edge, in the
back by the blackboard, wearing a jacket.

The sixth-grade teacher was a fiery-tempered redhead. Because she was an avid Brooklyn Dodgers fan, we listened to the whole World Series between the New York Yankees and Dodgers in class. She became distraught when the Dodgers lost, which was most of the time. She disappeared for a day or two to recover.

Having parents who owned a diner had its benefits, including our wonderful "brown bag" lunches, sometimes delivered to us at school. We opened our bags and pulled out meat loaf, roast beef, sausage and peppers, eggplant, and submarine sandwiches while most kids had peanut butter and jelly or bologna. We could tell how good the lunch was by the number of oil spots on the bag!

In the winter we each had a thermos of homemade soup — pea, navy bean, Manhattan clam chowder, tomato rice, or chicken noodle. The bag always included dessert, too, either a Danish, apple turnover, corn muffin, or a slice of Ms. Smith's pie (coconut custard, chocolate cream, lemon meringue, blueberry, or apple). When the teachers got word of our lunches, some ordered theirs from the diner and had it delivered to school.

Being aware of the diner's proximity, my sixth-grade teacher asked me to get her a sandwich and coffee for lunch and bring it back to the teacher's lunchroom. I got upset with her one day when she humiliated me in front of the class when I told a story.

My father went fly fishing with Harry Garbacio, the plumber, in Flat Brook. One day Harry caught a brook trout. As he reeled in the fish, the line broke. I told the class he went back the next day and caught the same fish, which still had his original hook and fly in its mouth.

"That was some fish story," our teacher commented to the class, implying it was far-fetched.

I thought about spitting in her coffee the next time I went to get her lunch. The angel on the one shoulder said, *Not nice! Don't do it!* The devil on the other side said, *Go ahead. She deserves it and will never know!* What do you think I did?

I also told the class about the field trip my father and I took to Uncle Charlie's workplace at the Erie Railroad train yard in Paterson. Uncle Charlie placed me in the cab of a diesel locomotive, moved it to a round table, rotated the table to a different set of tracks, and drove it to its storage facility. He also showed me an old steam locomotive. Quite an experience! The class really liked the story. No feedback from the teacher on that one.

Frankie Fiorella and I never forgot the day we went to the kindergarten class. He and I were in charge of delivering the white and chocolate milk cartons to every classroom in time for the afternoon cookie and milk break. When we entered the kindergarten, we saw the teacher slumped over to the right side of her chair as the children sat quietly at their desks. We ran back to our class and informed our teacher.

When the adults went to the kindergarten, they found that the teacher had passed away. I'm glad we found her quickly so the kindergartners didn't sit there for the rest of the day, not knowing what to do.

After-School Activities

Life during that time was much simpler. When dads returned from the war, many moms stayed at home and took care of the kids. We went to school, returned home, and changed our clothes. Most times we dressed in a polo shirt and dungarees, now called jeans. We put on our high-top Keds, the sneaker of choice, and went outside by ourselves to play war games in the woods or marbles, wall ball, or stickball behind Absalom Grundy School.

On holidays and weekends we left home in the morning and played all day long. No one was able to reach us because there were no cell phones, but they knew where we were. Even if we ate lots of cookies and cupcakes and drank soda with sugar, most of us weren't overweight because we were always outside playing.

Occasionally, we roller-skated with our skates attached to our sneakers. You needed a skate key to tighten your metal rollers to your sneakers or shoes. We either walked or rode our bikes (no helmet required) to these locations. When we cycled we put an elastic band or metal clip around our pant leg so our pants didn't get caught in the bike chain. Sometimes we attached Topps baseball cards to the spokes of the wheels with clothes pins to make a motor noise as he rode.

We personally collected baseball cards — all Yankees cards, some duplicates, some triples; most Brooklyn Dodgers; and some Giants. If we'd saved them, they'd be worth thousands of dollars today, but unfortunately they were thrown out after an attic cleaning.

We played in, on, and under the dirt. We had dirt on our bodies, under our fingernails, and on our clothing. No one we knew had allergies to anything. We drank water from a garden hose. And even though most of the dye houses in town dumped their silk dye wastewater into Molly Ann Brook, we fished and swam in it.

The Absalom Grundy School field had a large set of swings and a very high metal slide that became very hot in the summer. When we wore short pants, the slide burned our legs. When we hit bottom we slid right into the dirt and gravel, usually scraping our legs, but we survived and went down time after time. Our motto was, "Suck it up!"

We drew a good-sized circle in the dirt and placed eight to ten marbles in it. Our shooting marble was a clear agate called a "Puree." It was bigger than the rest. We knelt outside the ring and, using our thumb, flicked our shooting marble out of our fist. We aimed to hit as many of the other marbles out of the ring as possible. Most marbles were smooth and clear. Some of us liked to step on them and roll them back and forth on a concrete sidewalk to create a rough finish. That way, they were much easier to grip in the shooting position.

Sometimes we played "keepsie." In that game you kept any of your opponents' marbles that were knocked out of the ring.

Our other big game was stickball, a pick-up game sometimes called sandlot ball because, just like in Major League baseball, it was played on a baseball or softball field. Only our games, which usually went seven innings, were played with a broom handle and a rubber ball made by Spalding. The size of a tennis ball and hollow inside, it was called a "pink pearl" because of its color. We had fewer players than baseball—sometimes five per team. We also had no umps; on-deck players called balls and strikes. And we used mix-and-match rules from baseball or just made up our own.

We also used the pink ball for wall ball, a game in which one player serves: he hits the ball with an open hand so it bounces on the ground once before it reaches the school brick wall. The receiving player lets the ball hit the wall, bounce back, and hit the ground once before returning it. We took turns until someone missed. We kept count of the points we accumulated. If one player scored eleven straight points, the game ended. When players alternated in scoring points, the first to reach twenty-one won.

Eventually, we had to stop our activities because our family always ate dinner together, as did most families back then. Because the fields were close to our home, our father walked onto the front porch and, with his fingers on his lips, created a loud whistle we heard at the field. We ran home as fast as we could.

We also played a lot of football with no helmets and no face masks. That meant lots of bloody lips. Under the tutelage of Bart Dipaola, the Police Athletic League (PAL) ran some organized workouts. They even brought fire trucks down to the field with generators and lights so we could practice at night. Our best buddies on the team were Frank Fiorina, Jack Gamble, Gary Kamphouse, Jimmy Sees, Tony Santini, John Karpak, Alan Martichek, and too many others to name. We were very motivated to do well in football because our father and Uncle Elmer Gallo both played for the Haledon Hobarts, a well-known town football team. The original Hobarts started in 1931 with a donation from Garret Hobart, who, as mentioned earlier, was vice president under President McKinley. The Hobarts had a winning record from 1932 to 1939, scoring 1,220 points and giving up only 200. These were the impressive teams for which Dad and Uncle Elmer played.

Our fun was, as they say, good and clean. In those days the average person never used drugs such as marijuana or heroin. Some movie stars or jazz musicians did, but we only heard about it when they got caught.

Soap Box Derby

The American Legion sponsored the annual soap box derby that was run down Southside Avenue. We entered with the help of Uncle Elmer Gallo, who was a machinist. We built and designed the soap box, but he helped us construct an angle iron frame. Then we covered the frame with linoleum. Since I was the oldest of the boys, I was chosen to drive. The contestants had to run with the vehicle to start. I ran as fast I could but to no avail.

One of the other soap box entrants had bought official wheels from the National Soap Box Derby Association. So they smoked us going down the hill one-on-one. They won the three-speed bike prize.

Uncle Elmer's twin sons, Jimmy and Jerry—our cousins—were much younger than us. They drove the cart in future years.

Haledon PAL and Boxing

PAL organized and sponsored baseball teams, as we mentioned, but it also was active in boxing, music, and the shooting range. My brother and I and some friends were involved in all these sports.

The league event constructed a professional boxing ring in the Absalom Grundy School basement. One resident, Vince Martinez, was a boxer with a fast left hook and hard right hand. Though his surname was Spanish, he was Italian and very proud of his ancestry. Martinez was an uncrowned welterweight champion with a total of seventy-seven bouts — sixty-nine wins, eight losses, and thirty-six knockouts. Along with

Finamore family photo

Vince Martinez (center, without shirt) and the Haledon PAL boxing program. Standing third from left is Nick, and fifth from left is Bob.

many other qualified instructors, he helped teach us boxing skills. He lived on Granite Avenue, a block away from our Barbour Street home.

One of our friends who was slightly older, Frankie Aiello, became good enough to fight in the Golden Gloves. I fought him once. Though he only used one hand, he still was able to whiff by my chin with a lightning fast left hook. My guess is he didn't want to hurt me.

To encourage us, our parents bought a heavy punching bag and a high-speed punching bag so we could train at the house.

The season ended with a series of boxing rounds against other students matched according to age, weight class, and ability. A three-minute round of constant movement and action boxing was the most exhausting exercise we ever undertook, but we truly enjoyed it. Those boxing skills came in handy when I was a freshman in high school, which I'll cover later in this book.

Setting Bowling Alley Pins

Bob: In our day, before automatic pinsetters, bowling alleys had to be manually reset and the balls manually returned to bowlers. Nick and I worked as pin spotters at Joe Pipp's Bowling Lanes at an early age. We set for two alleys as two teams rolled three games of ten frames per game.

We sat at the end of the alley on an elevated partition that straddled each lane. Our wooden, bicycle-like seats were anchored atop the partition. Being high up and alongside the pit (the area where pins and balls accumulated) supposedly protected us from getting hit by flying pins. It didn't work. Every night we got hit in the lower torso. It was an occupational hazard.

If a bowler threw a strike, it was our job to place the ball on the return rails and reset all the pins. If the bowler didn't throw a strike, there were pins left standing. In that case we had to return the ball and clean the "dead wood"—the knocked-down pins— from the alley.

Pin replacement required a certain technique because it had to be quick. When replacing all ten pins, we stepped on a pedal in the pit, causing ten spike-like projections to emerge from the alley. They identified the proper location for the ten pins. Every pin had a hole centered at the bottom. We grabbed them by the narrow end at the top. With two pins in each hand, we quickly placed four pins in the correct position on the alley. We repeated the process for the next four. After positioning the last two, we hopped back up on our seat and prepared to repeat the same process in the other alley. Demanding work, but youth won the day!

Communion and Confirmation

We both received our First Holy Communion and Confirmation at Saint Paul's Roman Catholic Church on Haledon Avenue in Prospect Park, New Jersey — Communion in May 1949 and Confirmation in May 1953 at the ages of fourteen and thirteen.

For Communion, the nuns had us practice receiving the host using Necco Wafers, a hard disc candy the size of the Eucharist host. The object was not to chew the host and to wait until it melted in our mouth before we swallowed. When the time came for the sacrament, though, the actual host always found its way to the roof of our mouth and we always struggled to free it with our tongue so it wasn't torn or chewed.

We put an inordinate amount of preparation work into our confirmation. The prep was taught by nuns who wore habits — a black tunic hanging to the ground, scapulars over the tunic hanging both in front and back, and a white cotton cap.

We stayed after school in the church and memorized many questions and answers from the *Baltimore Catechism* such as: Who made us? Who is God? Why did God make you? What are the Stations of the Cross in order? What are the commandments in order? Recite the *Apostles' Creed*. We stayed until we could answer a set of questions assigned for that day. Only then were we dismissed. For some reason, the girls usually were more prepared than us boys, so they were allowed to leave earlier. A few of us had to remain until late in the evening. The nuns were always very nice to us.

It took me many years to understand the importance of developing a spiritual life along with a physical and mental one.

Finamore family photo

Nick (left) and Bob on the day of their First Holy Communion (1949).

Chapter 12
Music to Our Ears

My idol was my Uncle Al, the professional accordion player. He influenced me to take accordion lessons, which was fine with my mother. She decided that Bob was the "brawn" of the two of us, so it was decided that he take trumpet lessons.

I studied accordion at two music studios in downtown Paterson — Robbie's and Brino's, starting at age seven and lasting many years. Brino's had a show at the Majestic Theatre featuring thirty of us accordion players on stage.

Uncle Al was constantly traveling so he couldn't spend much time with me, but one time we got together for three hours in Astoria and he taught me plenty on that one occasion. An accomplished player, he performed on the *Lawrence Welk Show*. Welk, a bandleader and accordionist, hosted his television show more than thirty years. He featured a world-famous accordionist—Myron Floren, who was on stage all that time. In the '50s, though, Uncle Al was invited to perform with his trio, The Midnight Sons, on the show. It was quite an honor because Welk never had guest accordionists.

Uncle Al was supported by the Pancordion Company. He was a sponsor and advertised their instruments. In return, they provided him free accordions.

My brother and I were entered into a music contest for which famed radio personality Tiny Fairbanks was judge. First up, I played a solo entitled "Goodnight, Irene."

Bob: I was up next on trumpet. Accompanied by a pianist, I was going to play the "Sheik of Araby." As can happen occasionally, one of the three valves on my trumpet got stuck in the down position and I hit a wrong note in the middle of the song. I ran off the stage and stopped taking lessons.

Twin Brino daughters who played an accordion duet won the contest. They were invited to appear on the Fairbanks Radio Show.

The most logical reason for my stuck valve was a habit I had when practicing: if I had trouble hitting a note, I threw the trumpet against the basement wall. Patience was not one of my best virtues.

When I went to college, I took the trumpet with me. I got up early, before my football teammates were awake, and blew "Reveille" to awaken them for

practice. My teammates did not appreciate this act of kindness. One month when my personal funds were almost exhausted, I pawned the trumpet in downtown Memphis even though it had a bent valve and bell. I sold it for fifteen dollars at a Beale Street pawnshop. Our parents had bought it new and paid substantially more.

While our mother always emphasized a good education, she also wanted us to be involved with music. Even as a child she had wanted to take dancing lessons and become a professional dancer. So she often asked me to play the song "Tea for Two" on the accordion so she could do a tap dance — the heel toe shuffle step.

Striking Up The Band

Many of our new friends on the Barbour Street side of town took music lessons on different instruments — Tony Santini and Tommy Calamia on saxophone, Paul Caporossi on piano, Patsy Piccinnino on drums, and Jack Rock on guitar. Since I was studying accordion at Robbie's Music Studio in Paterson, it was natural for us to form a band.

When I was in sixth grade, we did. The Haledon PAL taught us how to play together as a unit. One of our primary teachers was Johnny Belvedere, an accordionist whose band, The Colt Combo, played at all the high school dances. The mascot of Paterson

Finamore family photo

Haledon PAL band. Members included (left to right) Tom Calamia, Jack Rock, Tony Santini, Ed Maskery, Pat Piccininno, Nick, and Paul Caporossi.

Central High School, which we attended several years later, is a colt. Therefore, the name of the group.

Johnny helped me become a better accordion player. And, along with others, he arranged for us to rehearse weekly at the Veterans Club building on Barbour Street. Our first gig was a PAL function at which our pianist, Paul Caporossi, sang "Blue Moon."

Later in elementary school, four of us broke off and started a smaller ensemble called The Sharps, which played through our years at Paterson Central High School. Later the group was called The Chessmen.

When I was in seventh and eighth grades, I found a new drummer by accident. In the summers of those years, I worked full time in the diner. During that period my mother took the opportunity to become a stay-at-home mom. Later she got involved in a business with Fran Ariola, her third cousin. Francine

Fashions was on Union Boulevard in the Totowa section of Paterson. To compensate for her absence, my dad hired Jimmy Iozia, a short order cook from Paterson in his late twenties. Jimmy was a wannabe drummer who played to the jukebox music with his open hands, pinkies up, on the counter.

THE SHARPS

Finamore family photo

The Sharps. Left to right: Tony Santini, saxophone; Joe Tamburro, bass; Pat Piccininno, drums, and Nick on accordion.

An Expanded Repertoire

Pat Piccinnino of The Sharps had left his drums set up in our basement at Barbour Street, where we often rehearsed. We also had an upright piano in the same rehearsal space.

I wanted to learn blind jazz pianist George Shearing's locked hands technique so I continuously played his versions of "I'll Remember April" and "September in the Rain." I became very proficient in this style. At that time, however, my real idol was pianist Bill Evans. Eventually, I patterned my style after his.

One day after work, I invited Jimmy to our home, where we played as a duo for hours.

Jimmy had many Paterson friends who knew the music of the day and brought sheet music to our band rehearsals. We learned "Night Train" and "Harlem Nocturne," two of the more popular hits. Our band played those songs for many years into the future.

I looked up to Jimmy and began to have my hair cut in the same style as his. I even started going to his barber, Sal Guerrero, who had a shop in downtown Paterson. The hairstyles then in vogue for men were a DA (for ducktail or duck's ass) and a TC (for Tony Curtis).

The DA was a slicked back style. Around the sides the hair was greased with pomade and parted down the back of the head and neck to look like a duck's ass. The TC, derived from Hollywood movie star Tony Curtis's coiffed locks, featured curls hanging down the forehead like a bunch of grapes. Elvis Presley copied that look. Anyone with that hairdo in the early '50s was called a greaser.

Chapter 13
Old School Ways

Our parents believed in discipline. Although we were never physically abused, we were sometimes spanked. Our mother and father threatened us with a leather barber's strap, twelve inches long and a quarter-inch thick, that they kept in the kitchen drawer. We didn't think of our mother as much of a threat.

We antagonized her when we got in trouble by laughing, running away, and hiding under our beds. She knelt down and swung the strap in an attempt to hit us. Sometimes we hid under a bed and she moved it to expose us. We simply slid from one twin bed to the other for cover.

"You are going to send me to Greystone!" she hollered, referring to a psychiatric hospital in Morris Plains, New Jersey.

One time frustration set in and she called our father at work. He came home in a fury because his workday had been disrupted. He picked up the two mattresses and beds we were hiding under, grabbed each of us by an arm, held us up, and hit us on the backside. Our mother panicked.

"Nick, you're going to kill them!" she yelled.

That was the last time our father doled out any corporal punishment. They were loving parents in all ways.

Bob: One Christmas our parents bought us bicycles as a surprise. But we'd discovered a small trap door in our bedroom closet floor that looked down into the basement. That Christmas Eve we faked sleep, got out of bed, and watched as they assembled the two bikes.

The next morning we opened a couple of the gifts. I received a Jerry Mahoney ventriloquist dummy, popular because of the Paul Winchell and Jerry Mahoney Show on TV. My brother got a microscope kit. After we opened a number of gifts, our parents announced there was something else downstairs.

"Oh, you mean the bikes?" we both said.

We were still thrilled with these bikes. I got a black-and-white "Hopalong Cassidy" bike, which had a holster and pistol in the connecting bar below the handlebars. Hopalong Cassidy was a popular TV cowboy heroes. Nick got a fancy gold and green Schwinn bike. We always received great gifts for

Christmas no matter how much money our parents had at the time. They were always generous to us.

Superstitions

We also lived with superstitions that were partially traditional and not necessarily Italian in origin. They were simply handed down through the generations and our family lore.

The first was the belief in an evil eye called *il Malocchio* (bad eye), pronounced "Maloik." If someone is jealous of another's good luck or fortune, they can place an evil eye on the other person. The evil eye is said to become a physical ailment, such as a headache, that can be brought on by a look. A person can ward off evil eyes by wearing a *cornetti* (red horn) resembling a chili pepper, usually around the neck. The horn was made of red coral because the color red was believed to have the strongest effect. Many people dangled the horn from the rearview mirror of their cars as a defense mechanism. Try explaining that when someone gets into the car: "Oh, that's so you don't get crippled."

The belief is an Old European tradition from when the horned animal (the moon goddess) was considered sacred. Its origins go back to the ancient Greeks and Romans and a famous saying, "If envy were fever, the whole world would be in bed." No one in our family was into the Old World negative power of envy but we had friends who followed that superstition.

Then there were two ways to ward off a curse. One was a protective hand gesture. If someone was speaking in a prideful way, you closed your hand in a fist and raised the forefinger and little finger, creating a pair of horns.

The other way was to place three drops of olive oil in a bowl of water. As the oil separated, the person performing the ritual cut through the oil and water with a large knife or pair of scissors. Our cousin Joan Alesso tells a story she remembers from her youth: She'd had a headache over many days so her mother, Aunt Ann Melone, jabbed a knife through the oil and water. Shortly thereafter, the headache disappeared.

Or maybe the Bayer aspirin finally worked.

Cure for Warts

Our Grandfather Carnevale performed a ritual to remove warts. My brother developed warts covering both hands. Afraid some people would recoil at feeling the rough warts, he found it difficult to shake hands with people. There were rumors then that people "caught" warts from handling toads or frogs, which brother Bob never did at that early age.

Bob: My grandfather took me to the Molly Ann Brook Bridge with a number of uncooked white cannellini beans, one for each wart on my hands. He rubbed a bean across each wart while he said, *Nel nome del Patre, il filio, e lo Spirito Santo, quando questi marchi marciscono, le verruche andranno.* **(In**

the name of the Father, the Son, and the Holy Spirit, when these beans rot, the warts will go away.) Then he threw the beans into the water. The theory was that the warts would disappear when the beans decayed or rotted.

Within a couple of weeks, the warts went away. My hands were completely clear. It turns out that warts caused by a virus usually disappear naturally in a few weeks to several years. Maybe the time was up!

We now know, too, that warts occur when the human papillomavirus (HPV) comes in contact with the skin or cuts in the skin. Children are more likely to get them because their immune systems aren't mature enough to ward off the virus.

We recall another strange incident based on a vivid dream our mother had one night. The next day she told the customers in the diner about it: She and our father were on the auto ferry that crossed the Hudson River. They were on their way to see our grandparents in Astoria, Queens. On the way she dropped her purse, containing a substantial amount of cash, overboard. She told my father, who dived into the water to retrieve the purse. He was successful. Then he was pulled from the water with a life jacket and brought back onto the ferry.

One customer overheard her telling the story.

"There's a dream book that translates dream images into numbers," he said. "You should figure out the numbers and play them with a local bookie."

Based on the images she dreamed, our mother did just that. To our surprise, she won four hundred dollars, a rather large sum in those days.

Chapter 14
Young Men

After we advanced to seventh grade, we went back across town to the Kossuth Street School, built in 1895. It had a bell tower. Some student was selected to pull down on a long heavy twisted rope and ring the bell in the morning. We found that if we held onto the rope, we could ride up a number of feet into the air although that was strictly prohibited. When no one was looking, we took the risk, though. There was just too much temptation and fun involved to obey that rule.

We walked or rode our bikes back and forth from Barbour Street to school in the morning, at lunchtime, and after school. Because all students had to cross main thoroughfares such as Belmont and Haledon avenues, the school district formed a program called "The Junior Patrol." Each school had a squad with a captain, lieutenants, patrolmen, and substitutes. They

Courtesy of American Labor Museum / Botto House National Landmark
Kossuth Street School.

alternated daily in covering their assigned post. Teachers nominated students in the higher grades to stand at major intersections and assist younger students to safely cross. We higher-grade kids wore bright white belts, three inches wide, that went from one shoulder diagonally across our backs and around our waists. The captain wore a yellow belt. Very visible! I was nominated captain two years in a row. My job was to assure that all positions were covered and find a substitute if someone was missing.

One day I got into trouble because I went to school early on my bike and passed an unoccupied position that I should have filled. I had assumed the assigned student would be there later. A parent noticed and reported it. Mr. McRae, junior patrol adviser, and Miss Stansfield, the principal, scolded me for that safety violation but there was no punishment. The unoccupied position was supposed to be manned by one of my junior patrol classmates. I should have known better.

Miss Stansfield, a very tall, intimidating, and dominating figure with glasses, was the principal for both schools though her main office was at Kossuth Street. We were very frightened of her authority. I don't recall her ever smiling or laughing. She ran the schools as "tight ships" but was very smart and savvy.

Once Jack Rock and I were asked to perform as a duo on stage—him on guitar, me on accordion—at an assembly of all students from kindergarten through eighth grade. We started the song. Halfway through I had a mental block and froze as my face turned red. I kept hitting all the wrong notes. Miss Stansfield was standing at the rear of the auditorium.

"Start over!" she calmly shouted out.

We did, and Jack and I got through to the end without a hitch the second time. She saved me on a major school embarrassment that day!

Bob and I did get in trouble another time, though. One weekend the neighborhood boys found that the black metal coal shoot door behind Absalom Grundy School was open. A bunch of us crawled in. We were able to get into the school through the basement. One boy went to the second floor and ransacked the copy room, throwing papers all over the room. Bob and I were not part of that, but on Monday Miss Stansfield called me into her office.

"How was your weekend?" she asked me.

"It was good," I replied, not thinking much about it.

"Anything eventful?"

"Not that I can think of."

She dismissed me for the time being and brought down the other neighborhood boys to her office. She knew what took place but not knowing exactly what had happened or who was involved. Later she called me to her office again to confront me. It was clear she knew I was there, so I admitted I'd gone into the school but said I hadn't done anything destructive.

By interrogating all the boys, Miss Stansfield eventually uncovered the details of the whole episode and who did what. Having gathered enough other evidence, she believed me. There was no punishment, just a stern reprimand and a directive not to do anything like that again.

Pretty Girls

We had many pretty girls at school, including Joan DeBlock, Celia Pelosi, Lois Sinkway, Doris Wallerius, Peggy Worflar, Francis (Chi Chi) Andolino, Mabel Fiorina, Mary Ann Scrobolski, and many others we skated with. When one of our friends had a seventh- or eighth-grade birthday party, we played kissing games—our first real adventures with the opposite sex.

One such party game was Spin the Bottle. We all sat in a circle. A bottle was placed on the floor in the center. A person spun the bottle and then had to kiss the person to whom the bottle pointed when it stopped.

In the Post Office game, one person chosen by the group went outside and knocked on a door. Another person was chosen to answer the door and pay for the "letter" with a kiss. There were many variations on this game.

At formal dances the boys usually stood on one side of the room and the girls on the other. To help this situation, the school brought in a dance instructor. After school she taught us the basic dances of that time—the Foxtrot, Waltz, and Tango. Knowing what to do really helped on the next dance outing.

Wood Shop

Mr. McRae, our fantastic shop teacher who was proud of his Scottish heritage, taught us how to build our own wood or wrought iron projects. In our beginning seventh-grade classes, though, the first order of business was building a wood birdhouse. We were introduced to tools like a coping saw, hammer, and screwdriver.

In eighth grade we built much larger, sophisticated projects that took the entire school year to complete—

end tables, large desks, and iron lamps, for instance. During these projects, we learned to use a circular table saw, planer, sander, and other electrical and mechanical tools. Mr. McRae taught us to safely operate these electrical tools.

Bob: Mr. McRae taught me the proper way to clean a paint/stain/varnish can. When we finished painting, he told us to run a rag or towel around the reservoir at the top until it was clean. In my entire life as a do-it-yourselfer, I've always used this method. Additionally, when closing the lid, I place a rag or towel over the top and use a hammer to beat down around the rim. No splatter! And next time I use the paint, the can is easier to open — no mess, no rust!

Mr. McRae was very particular regarding tool storage. A large plywood board hung on the shop wall. It contained painted shadow figures that outlined each specific tool — hammer, chisel, screwdriver, and all the other handheld tools. Over the board hung a sign that read, "A place for every tool and every tool in its place." Before each class ended, we made sure all tools were hung and the board was visibly filled correctly. This graphic has stuck with Nick and me when we organize anything. We have repeated this saying frequently over our lifetimes.

The other part of Mr. McRae's class, mechanical drawing, attracted me. We performed detailed drawings in each isometric view and dimension. The class always felt like a competitive contest in who could finish a drawing first and be signed off by Mr.

McRae. He got annoyed when submittals were very sloppy and refused to sign off on them until their quality was improved.

Mr. McRae suspended a variety of model planes from the shop ceiling with string—a B29 aircraft, B17 Flying Fortress, P40 "Flying Tiger," and many more Kawasaki and Mitsubishi Japanese planes. German *Luftwaffe* aircraft were also included.

During World War II Mr. McRae was tasked with teaching his students to build these models, which were then used to train our pilots to recognize enemy aircraft as well as our own. As far as we could determine, he had the premier woodshop of any elementary school in the area. We received an outstanding education in woodworking that has served us well through the years.

Bob: One day Mr. McRae was enraged in class. One of our classmates was making a knife blade out of a piece of metal on the grinding machine. Mr. McRae grabbed him by the arm and herded him out of class. He was so angry, his face was beet red. He walked behind the individual as he escorted him out of the shop.

Another time he came into class visibly upset because three eighth-graders had been shooting BB rifles at each other. The BB air gun shoots small metallic ball projectiles, sometimes called bottle washers, with high velocity. One of the students was hit in the eyelid. The muscle was injured severely.

Mr. McRae was so concerned that he invited the boy into class to discuss what had happened and show us his eye. The sight left an enduring impact on me and the class. The boy's eyelid was permanently closed for life because a BB pellet had impaired a nerve.

This story brings to mind another toy technology we used to hit and annoy each other. We blew small dried peas through straws, making the peas into projectiles. Pea shooting was certainly annoying but not nearly as dangerous as the BB gun.

Eighth-Grade Teachers

One teacher sold her mother's homemade raisin bread at school—with administrative and parental permission, of course. Today that would be a conflict of interest.

Our eighth-grade homeroom teacher, Mr. Mazzerina, was a very large man who weighed at least three hundred pounds. He was a great mentor for that age group. For example, before the school year ended, he asked Tony Santini and me our summer vacation plans. Both of us wanted to build our strength, so we told him we wanted to work on a farm.

Mr. Mazzerina drove us to the country. We stopped whenever we saw a farmer and asked if they were hiring for that summer. Though he drove us many miles and we made many stops, we didn't land a job. So it was back to the family diner business for me.

Our other teacher for eighth grade was Miss Hamer, who shared teacher duties on some subjects. She was very demanding. In English class she taught us how to

Finamore family photo

Kossuth Street School class of 1953. Teachers, back row: Mr. McRae at left and Mr. Mazzerina next to him; Miss Stansfield, center; and Miss Hamer, second from right. Nick is in the fourth row from the bottom, fourth from the left.

Finamore family photo

Kossuth Street School class of 1954. Teachers, back row (L-R): Mr. McRae, Miss Stansfield, Mr. Mazzerina, and Miss Hamer. Bob is in the fourth row from the bottom, second from right.

diagram sentences with great proficiency. We were drilled over and over. To this day I'm very comfortable with subjects and predicates, adverbs, adjectives, pronouns, and more.

Throughout our elementary school education, we were taught the basic Rs — reading, 'riting, and 'rithmetic, including cursive handwriting.

Future Farmers of America

In 1953 I started my freshman year at Paterson Central High School. Every day I took a public bus down to Paterson. The Haledon elementary schools were considered to be of high academic excellence, and I'd gotten very good grades, so I wanted to continue that level of achievement in the new school. Among my first classes as a freshman was a particular English class. I remember all the details vividly because, you know, that's how it is with any traumatic event.

As I sat at my desk, trying to pay attention to the teacher, two students behind me on my left side talked loudly to each other. I turned to them.

"Can you be quiet?" I asked. "I'm trying to concentrate."

"Who are you to tell us what we can do?" one replied. My next remark was spontaneous.

"Come outside," I said, "and I'll take both of you at one time!"

I was a little skinny kid about 145 pounds. I didn't want any trouble, so I forgot about it. In the cafeteria that day I sat with a large number of friends and upper classmates, some of them seniors and juniors from Haledon.

Suddenly I was surrounded by twenty Future Farmers of America (FFA) students. The FFA is a youth organization that promotes and supports agricultural education. I realized later that they were looked down upon as a group. They probably felt marginalized. There were eighteen hundred kids in the school and thirty to forty members of the FFA. The scenario was city slickers versus farmers.

"We heard you wanted to fight any two of us," their leader said.

"I only had a problem in class with two of you talking," I said. "I don't want any trouble. I don't want to fight anybody."

But they kept antagonizing me. The leader was the only female in the FFA group. A lot of my Haledon friends egged me on.

"Come on, Nick, go ahead," they said. "Nick, Come on, go ahead. You know you can take these two guys." Finally, I caved in because I didn't want to look like a wimp.

Our high school was across the street from the Passaic County Courthouse where many students went at lunchtime or during the day to watch trials. A large group of Haledonites and FFA members, as well as many other students who'd gotten the word about the fight, walked behind the courthouse. It was a cold fall day in September.

"Pick any two of us!" said one guy from the FFA.

"I don't have a problem with any others but these two were loud in class," I replied.

I immediately remembered *Amboy Dukes*, a book I'd recently read about a street gang in Perth Amboy, New Jersey. In a fight in the book, a gang member said, "Wait a minute" before the fight ensued.

"Wait a minute, let me take off my jacket," I said, taking a page from the book. I suppose my boxing training came into play, too, as I started to take my jacket off. Instead I swung twice very quickly and hit both my opponents in the face, knocking them down. They started to cry. I realized all the FFA members were humiliated. I put on my jacket and walk away, thinking that was the end of that.

As I walked away, though, one of the other big farmers came up to me.

"I'll take you one on one, you know. You want to fight?" Another group approached.

"Don't even think about coming to the school tomorrow," they said. "You're in big trouble and we are going to kill you after school tomorrow."

I didn't take that literally. I thought they'd gang up on me and beat me up. As I bused home, I shook. I was a new kid in the school. I didn't want any trouble.

The next day I talked to all my buddies from Haledon. They said they'd keep me safe after school.

Then they spread the word about the situation throughout the high school.

"I think our friend Nick is going to be in trouble," I heard one say. "You know, the farmers are after him." One of the kids they recruited was "Footsie" Clifton, a basketball player about six foot six, so nicknamed because he had large feet. All day they recruited a large number of their network, including seniors, as word circulated throughout the school.

At the end of the day they told me to go out the front door, which was about thirty feet from the curb and street. When I left two lines of students and friends faced each other, leaving space between the lines, which extended right to the curb. A car, its door open, waited for me in the street. A group of about thirty FFA students stood together and observed on the sidelines as I was escorted through the phalanx-like formation of students and friends.

I walked between the two lines and got into the car. They drove me home. Whew! I didn't have another problem with the FFA after they saw that show of force. They were no match for the camaraderie and reach of the Haledon kids.

The Rest of Our Lives

Nick

As I put the beginning of my high school freshman year behind me, I turned to my academics and a number of extracurricular activities for my remaining four years.

Bob and I were starters on the football team where I played right tight end on the line and he played next to me as a tackle—until he broke his wrist during my senior year. That year we had a winning record. In front of more than ten thousand fans who filled Hinchcliffe Stadium to capacity, we managed to beat our crosstown rival, Paterson Eastside High School, in the annual Thanksgiving classic. Being selected by my teammates as the Most Valuable Player (MVP) for that 1957 season was one of the highest honors of my life.

In the days before the big game there was a standing tradition: players signed students' programs in the cafeteria during lunch. One of those days a little cheerleader named Marie DeFabrizio asked me to sign my name and "15," my jersey number, under my photo in her program. She has her own version of that story, but that's for another book. And that's how I met my wife. As of this writing, we are married fifty-seven years and have three children and six grandchildren.

My music career continued with The Sharps, the four-piece rock and roll combo. I played the accordion with my Haledon boyhood musician friends, Tony on sax and Pat on drums. We added Joe Tamburro, a bass player. The Sharps played at most of the high school dances held in the gymnasium with low colored lights — a scene right out of the movie *Back to the Future*.

Later I transitioned to The Chessmen, a five-piece jazz band, and switched to piano and B3 organ. We played weddings, parties, and New Jersey nightclubs on weekends until 1965 when I left the music scene to focus on my AT&T career.

The other hobby that gave me life direction was getting my ham radio license when I was sixteen. I built twenty-four Heathkit do-it-yourself electronic kits, including many receivers and transmitters for my K2QDS amateur radio station. My love for this hobby was instrumental in my decision to pursue an electrical engineering degree.

After high school I attended the University of Miami in Coral Gables, Florida and majored in engineering for one year. The tuition was a whopping four hundred dollars per semester. I then came home, where I commuted from our home in Wayne, New Jersey and attended Newark College of Engineering

(NCE), which later changed its name to the New Jersey Institute of Technology (NJIT). Tuition there was two hundred dollars per semester. In 1962 I graduated with a bachelor of science degree in electrical engineering. That same year Marie and I wed at Saint John's Cathedral in Paterson with Bob as my best man. All The Chessmen and Marie's cousins were in the bridal party — sixteen in all.

I'd begun my career at Western Electric Company (AT&T) a year earlier and had assignments of increasing authority throughout my thirty-four years in the areas of engineering, computer systems, sales, and human resources. Over time I learned that the people in the company are our most important asset.

When I retired in 1995, New Jersey Governor Christie Whitman recruited me as a "loaned executive" to help the government improve its operations. AT&T funded me for this assistance. I left twelve years later. My most significant contribution was helping the New Jersey Motor Vehicle Commission become more customer- and citizen-focused and adopt a quality orientation that cut down wait times and improved its processes.

Another major project was assisting Phil Scanlan, the AT&T vice president of quality, and the State Department of Environmental Protection clean up the ocean along the many miles of the seashore. What? The claim in 1989 was that New York was polluting New Jersey seawater. With a root cause and quality analysis, we concluded the one hundred forty communities along the shoreline were the ones really at fault. Phil's book, *The Dolphins Are Back: A Successful Quality Model for Healing the Environment*, detailed exactly how. It also explained what was accomplished over ten years to make the New Jersey seashore the cleanest in the nation, as measured at the time. Quite a story! It was and continues to be a best-kept secret.

In 1976 Marie and I made a significant decision to move our family to Boston, Massachusetts when AT&T asked me to help start a sales office there. We thought it would be a two-year rotational assignment. We stayed for thirteen years until I was transferred, after four promotions, back to New York as regional vice president for the company's Northeastern region.

The move to Massachusetts, however, had its benefits. Our three children had the opportunity and good fortune to meet their life partners and brought us the joys of a lifetime as we watched our six grandchildren grow and mature on the beaches of Old Silver Beach on Buzzards Bay in Cape Cod.

I realize now that my morals and values — honor, pride, self-respect, and patriotism — were mainly passed down to us at family gatherings with parents, grandparents, other family members, and friends. In current days technology and the media play a much larger role. Unfortunately, the secular world doesn't always communicate what we believe. My boyhood in this small town of Haledon and close family relationships instilled in me a strong work ethic, physical and mental disciplines, and many other family values. Trying to live these personal qualities made it possible for me to become a happy and fulfilled husband, father, grandfather and businessman.

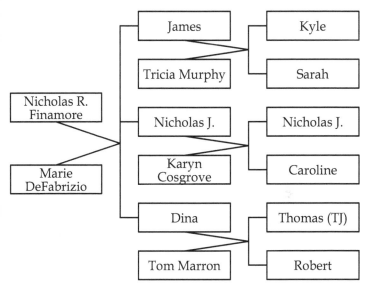

Nick's descendants.

Bob

Sports had a formative influence on my life from the start. My interests were always in physical activities and organized sports. At Paterson Central High School, which I entered in 1954, I became a three-year varsity starter on the football team and a four-year starter on the baseball team.

During my senior year I was one of the captains in football. This was the year (1957) that the H2N2 Virus pandemic caused the cancellation of three of our football games. At the end of that 1957 season my teammates voted me Most Valuable Player (MVP). Our end-of-year football banquet, held at the Brownstone in Paterson, also included the Eastside High School football team. Frank Gifford, star running back for the New York Giants, was the guest speaker. Bill Galese, who became my mentor and very good friend, received the MVP for Eastside High School. Gifford signed both our trophies.

Bill and I were both recruited by Ray Malavasi, a native of Clifton, New Jersey, to play Division I college football at Memphis State University in Memphis, Tennessee. Before and after his coaching stint at Memphis State, Ray coached for Minnesota, Wake Forest, the Denver Broncos and the Los Angeles Rams.

At Memphis State I was a four-year starting offensive guard and a noseguard on defense. At the end of my senior year my teammates voted me MVP. I was also selected to play in the 1964 Blue-Gray Classic in Montgomery, Alabama. Sportswriters selected me as the Defensive MVP for the Gray Squad.

I was drafted as a free agent by the New York Jets in 1965. After the Jets released me I finished the season with the Newark Bears of the Continental Football League. When Tommy Granatell, the owner, decided to move the team to Orlando, Florida, they became the Orlando Panthers. I received my new contract and was ready to sign it. Before the 1966 season began, however, I received my draft notice from the US Defense Department.

During a summer respite from college, I was fortunate to have met a very attractive Natalie Woods look-alike at the home of my sister-in-law's parents. Shirley Ann Belmont and I married on January 8, 1966.

Ten days later, on January 18, 1966, at age twenty-six, I was on a bus headed to Fort Dix, New Jersey for basic training. There was a war in Vietnam. So despite being newly married and having the opportunity to continue my football career, I was comfortable putting my life on hold for two years as I fulfilled my military obligation. Many of my family members had served in the military. I felt, as they did, that service and patriotism are part of the fabric of our country and essential to the survival of a democratic society.

Shirley spent the last year of my enlistment with me at Fort Bliss, Texas. We returned to New Jersey after I was discharged and settled in our new hometown of Wayne, New Jersey.

When I returned home after my discharge, my college teammate and friend Bill Galese invited me to join him at Eastside High School in 1968. We worked together, teaching and coaching, for the next twenty-five years. After Eastside, I worked at Elmwood Park (East Paterson) High School, Morris Hills High School, and Manchester Regional High School. Bill became a head coach and/or administrator at all these schools.

I retired in 2005 after thirty-five years of service, having earned two years' credit for my service time. Shirley and I were married for forty-four years until she passed away in 2008. We had two children and two grandchildren.

Someone once said, "Life is a journey that must be traveled no matter how bad the roads and accommodations." All my endeavors—early days in Haledon, adolescent days in high school, college, military service, marriage, fatherhood, and grandparenting—have been challenging. Yet each has individually brought me much joy and gratification. My long, successful journey would not have been possible without the discipline, strong work ethic, perseverance, values, and resilience instilled in me by my family and the many friends I met along the way.

I may not have gone where I intended to go, but I've ended up where I needed to be.

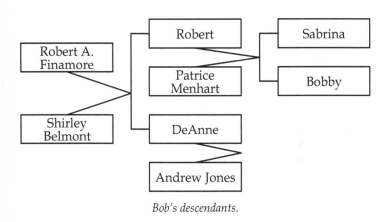

Bob's descendants.

Family Recipes

Grandma Finamore's Scarola (Escarole) and Beans

Ingredients

3 bags of fresh chopped and cleaned escarole or, in Italian, *scarola*

1 can (15 oz.) of Campbell's pork and beans or cannellini beans

3 cloves of garlic, chopped

3 tbsps. extra virgin olive oil

½ tsp. salt and pepper each

Pinch of red pepper flakes

Directions

1. Sauté garlic in a large frying pan with heated oil until transparent.

2. Add escarole a little at a time as it cooks down until all is incorporated and completely wilted.

3. Continue sautéing 10 to 15 minutes until the consistency is firmer or softer escarole as desired.

4. Add beans with the liquid and heat through.

5. Add pepper flakes, salt, and pepper to taste.

Grandma Carnevale's Pasta Fagioli

Ingredients

4-6 sausage links — sweet or hot or combination — 1–1½ lbs.

Extra virgin olive oil

1 small onion, chopped

6 cloves of garlic, chopped

1 16-oz. can of cannellini beans, undrained

2 lb. 3 oz. can of crushed tomatoes

8 ozs. Ditalini Pasta (parboiled)

2 cans of beef broth

Directions

1. In a soup pot or Dutch oven, chop sausage (use 3 hot and 3 sweet links, 1 to 1½ lbs., with removed skin) into small pieces while browning in olive oil. Remove and set aside. Add more oil, if necessary, and sauté a small chopped onion and 6 cloves of chopped garlic. Add a 16-oz. can of white cannellini beans, undrained, with fresh parsley, basil, and oregano (2 tbsp. each plus 1 tsp. salt and ½ tsp. of pepper) to taste. Simmer for 5 minutes. Add a 2 lb. 3 oz. can of crushed tomatoes and return meat to pot. Simmer another 15 minutes.

2. Add 8 oz. parboiled Ditalini pasta and simmer, adding 2 cans of beef broth gradually. It will thicken so continue adding broth. Cook until the pasta reaches an ideal texture. Before serving sprinkle with parmesan cheese

Note: Don't overcook parboiled pasta. It will soften in final stages of cooking with other ingredients in pot.

Dad's Texas Weiner Chili Sauce

Ingredients

1 lb. chopped meat

29-oz. can tomato sauce

2 cups of water

1 tsp. salt

1 tsp. pepper

2–3 tsps. chili powder

1 tbsp. Gravy Master or Kitchen Bouquet

⅔ cup of bread crumbs

Directions

1. Break up 1 lb. chop meat and place in a large pot and cover with 2 cups of water. Boil for 3 to 4 minutes and then add a 29-oz. can of tomato sauce along with 1 tsp. salt, 1 tsp. pepper, 2 to 3 tsps. of chili powder, and 1 tbsp. of Gravy Master or Kitchen Bouquet.

2. Hold out ⅔ cup of bread crumbs. Simmer for about 30 minutes, occasionally adding in bread crumbs to thicken sauce as needed to obtain a thick consistency.

Mom's Sunday Gravy

Ingredients

1 medium onion, chopped

2 cloves garlic, chopped

2 to 4 tbsps. extra virgin olive oil

2½ tsps. dried basil

¼ cup chopped fresh flat leaf parsley

2 tsps. salt

½ tsp. black pepper

2 large cans crushed tomatoes

1 large can of tomato sauce or 2 cans of tomato paste (with 4 cans of water)

12 meatballs (recipe separate)

1 package of sweet Italian sausages

1 package of pork *braciole* (package already seasoned and rolled or another recipe included)

Directions

1. Heat half the oil in a large heavy pot over medium heat and brown the sausage and braciola, one package at a time.

2. In a separate frying pan brown the meatballs.

3. After all the meat has been browned remove from pot and add the rest of the oil. Saute the onion for about 5 minutes and add garlic and continue to sauté for another 2 minutes.

4. Add crushed tomatoes and all other ingredients. Stir and simmer together over low heat for 15 minutes.

5. Add all the meat and stir carefully until all is covered by the sauce. Let simmer, uncovered on low heat, for 1½ hours, stirring frequently so as not to burn the bottom of the pot.

Mom's Italian Meatballs

Ingredients

1 lb. ground beef or combination of beef, veal and pork

¼ cup fresh basil

2 large eggs

⅓ cup grated parmigiano-reggiano cheese

¼ cup fresh chopped parsley

¼ cup extra virgin olive oil

All purpose flour

2 slices of bread with crust cut off (in those days white Wonder Bread soaked in milk)

1 cup of bread crumbs

2 tbsps. extra virgin olive oil

Garlic powder

Salt and pepper to taste — approximately ¼ tsp. each

Directions

1. In a large bowl place the ground meat, eggs, and bread and all other ingredients. Slowly add the bread crumbs and mix with your clean hands until well blended and to get a firm consistency.

2. Take small portions and roll together to form meatballs about 1½ inches.

3. Coat the meatballs with flour and breadcrumbs until lightly but evenly coated. Heat ¼ cup olive oil in a large heavy skillet over medium high heat. Slip as many meatballs into the skillet as can fit, turning to brown on all sides.

4. Drop the meatballs in the sauce (other recipe) when simmering for 1½ hours.

Mom's Stuffed Eggplant Parmesan

Ingredients

1 large eggplant (peeling optional)

3 or more tbsps. extra virgin olive oil

3 eggs

4 slices of white, wheat, or Italian bread (discard crusts)

2 tbsps. grated parmesan cheese

2 tbsps. snipped flat-leaf parsley

1 tsp. chopped fresh basil

¼ tsp. salt

¼ tsp. pepper

Tomato sauce — homemade or favorite jar

Sliced mozzarella cheese

Directions

1. Cut eggplant lengthwise into ½-inch slices. Place the slices in a colander over a large bowl or pot underneath. Put a kitchen dishcloth over the eggplant and place a heavy iron or skillet on top to weigh it down. This process helps drain and squeeze out all the moisture and bitter juice in the eggplant. This leaves the eggplant less over-the-

top bitter and more sweet and pure. All Italian grandmothers know this.

2. Cover bottom of deep fry pan with oil (3 tbsp. extra virgin olive oil) and fry eggplant in pairs on one side. Turn one cooked slice over and add a layer of stuffing on top (see stuffing recipe).

3. Place second eggplant slice on top with uncooked side up. Turn the eggplant sandwich over after the bottom slice is browned. Place stuffed eggplant sandwiches on paper towel.

4. In a casserole, lay stuffed slice sandwiches on bottom, cover with tomato sauce (homemade or favorite jar — Victoria or Rao's) and grated parmesan cheese and repeat layers (two or three) until all of the eggplant is placed in casserole. Bake at 350 degrees for 20 to 30 minutes. You can melt slices of mozzarella cheese on top.

Stuffing

Combine 3 beaten eggs in a large bowl with 4 slices of bread (cut off four ends on each slice of white or wheat or Italian bread without the crust), 1 tbsp. of grated parmesan cheese, snipped parsley (2 tbsp. flat leaf), basil (1 tsp. chopped fresh) and salt and pepper. Mix the bread and eggs with hands until it holds together in a stuffing consistency.

Acknowledgments

While writing this book, Bob and I went back and forth many times to jog long-lost memories of our childhood in Haledon. However, many others complemented these recollections and refined many of our anecdotes. Most notably, our cousins Ray Finamore and Joan Allesso reminded us of much information about our Grandma Finamore, a special caring person always concerned about doing for others. Joan lived with her and Ray visited her often over the years and became very close to her, as we did.

A special thanks is extended to Lou and Peggy Coral who filled in many blanks on the Haledon environment. They also helped us remember many of the townspeople. Lou confirmed and enhanced many memories we had regarding delivering newspapers through his business.

Thank you, Jim O'Kane, for sharing your book about your boyhood in Brooklyn. After I told him a story from my childhood at our early morning breakfast meetings, Jim encouraged me to "write it down." He was emphatic that we should write the book. Jim also read the original manuscript and provided a wealth of valuable insights to help us develop and refine the writing.

Grateful thanks are extended to DeAnne and Andrew Finamore-Jones, who next pushed us to do a Q&A video recording, and then converted the audio into text to give us a strong foundation to begin the writing. They did much additional work along the way, including enhancing and accessing photos and developing an artist's conception of the Belmont Diner.

We owe an enormous credit to Lorraine Ash, our editor, for first performing the heavy lift of charting our raw manuscript and then doing the line-by-line musical line editing. She had warm patience with all the changes and edits we made during that process.

Thanks are also extended to Bill Ash of their Cape House Books publishing company. He pulled it all together with Lorraine to ready the book for self-publishing.

A nod to Evelyn M. Hershey, education director of the Botto House Museum, and to Allen Susen, Haledon municipal clerk/administrator, for helping us obtain many historic photos of Haledon.

A special thank you to Clare Ferraro, former president of Viking Press, who read and critiqued the original raw manuscript and encouraged us after publication to do an audiobook using our own voices.

Acknowledgments

Great appreciation to Marie's brother, Nick DeFabrizio, former teacher and vice principal at Central and Kennedy high schools, for confirming our memories and descriptions of Haledon characters. He also filled in and refined some historical facts. Thanks also to Marie's sister, Judy Ventrella, for hosting and facilitating this luncheon get-together.

Finally, we extend thanks to our sons Rob, Nick, and Jim and our daughters Dina and DeAnne, who put up with all our boyhood stories from the good old days.

Notes

1. *Haledon: 100 Years of History, 1908-2008* (Haledon Centennial Book Committee, 2012).

2. Immobiliare Caserio, "Fraine Abruzzo Hills," accessed April 23, 2020, https:// www.resources.immobiliarecaserio.com/the-village-of-fraine-in-the-region-of-abruzzo-chieti-province/

3. *Haledon: 100 Years of History, 1908-2008* (Haledon Centennial Book Committee, 2012).

4. Linda Everett, *Retro Diner: Comfort Food from the American Roadside* (Portland: Collectors Press, 2002), 5-6.

5. John Baeder, *Diners* (New York: Harry N. Abrams, Inc., 1978, 1995), 13.

6. Michael C. Gabriele, *The History of Diners in New Jersey* (Charleston: American Palate, 2013), 25.

7. Richard J. S. Gutman, *American Diner: Then and Now* (Baltimore: Johns Hopkins University Press, 2000), 12, 14, 53, 54, 58, 82.

8. Baeder, *Diners*, 12.

9. Leah Koenig, "Lost foods of New York City: Charlotte Russe," *Politico*, February 6, 2012, https://www.politico.com/states/new-york/albany/story/2012/02/lost-foods-of-new-york-city-charlotte-russe-067223.

10. Leah Koenig, "Lost Foods of New York City: Biscuit Tortoni," *Politico*, June 13, 2012, https://www.politico.com/states/new-york/albany/story/2012/06/lost-foods-of-new-york-city-biscuit-tortoni-067223.

11. Ralph Ventre, "Retiring His Whistle: Edgar Cartotto...A Half Century As An Educator, Mentor & Officiating Icon," Northeast Conference, accessed April 23, 2020, https://northeastconference.org/news/2009/3/10/mbb-edgarcartottofeature.aspx.

12. Laura Schumm, "America's Patriotic Victory Gardens," History Channel, accessed April 23, 2020, https://www.history.com/news/americas-patriotic-victory-gardens.

13. World History Project, "Babe Ruth is diagnosed with a malignant tumor in his neck," accessed April 23, 2020, https://worldhistoryproject.org/1946/11/babe-ruth-is-diagnosed-with-a-malignant-tumor-in-his-neck.